BASICS
MARKETING

Brian Sheehan

03

Marketing management

Ethical: aware-
ness/
reflect-
ion/
debate

academia

An AVA Book

Published by AVA Publishing SA
Rue des Fontenailles 16
Case Postale
1000 Lausanne 6
Switzerland
Tel: +41 786 005 109
Email: enquiries@avabooks.com

Distributed by Thames & Hudson (ex-North America)
181a High Holborn
London WC1V 7QX
United Kingdom
Tel: +44 20 7845 5000
Fax: +44 20 7845 5055
Email: sales@thameshudson.co.uk
www.thamesandhudson.com

Distributed in the USA & Canada by:
Ingram Publisher Services Inc.
1 Ingram Blvd.
La Vergne TN 37086
USA
Tel: +1 866 400 5351
Fax: +1 800 838 1149
Email: customer.service@ingrampublisherservices.com

English Language Support Office
AVA Publishing (UK) Ltd.
Tel: +44 1903 204 455
Email: enquiries@avabooks.com

ISBN 978-2-940411-51-1

Library of Congress Cataloging-in-Publication Data
Sheehan, Brian.
Basics Marketing 03: Marketing Management/Brian Sheehan p. cm.
Includes bibliographical references and index.
ISBN: 9782940411511 (pbk.:alk.paper)
eISBN: 9782940447282
1.Marketing.2.Marketing--Study and teaching.
HF5415 .S544 2011

10 9 8 7 6 5 4 3 2 1

Design by David Shaw

Production by AVA Book Production Pte. Ltd., Singapore
Tel: +65 6334 8173
Fax: +65 6259 9830
Email: production@avabooks.com.sg

Don Draper of *Mad Men*
Popular images of marketing executives often belie the importance of visionary leadership, the need for comprehensive strategic skills and the sensitivity to deal with delicate personnel issues. Management stereotypes are best avoided.

Table of contents

This book about management skills for marketing people holds special importance for me. While my first book about the basics of online marketing explored a growing new field of marketing, this book is more personal. It is the book that I wish someone had written for me when I stepped into my first management position in marketing.

As a manager, I suddenly had responsibilities far beyond the normal advertising campaign planning I was used to. Now I was also responsible for financial planning, corporate budgets, our competitive business strategy and managing a large number of employees (along with their myriad human resources issues). Later, when I was made CEO of Saatchi & Saatchi Advertising, Japan, I became responsible for setting the company's course and inspiring everyone in the company to move in that direction. I also had to deal with crisis management and creating an ethical corporate culture. Little in my previous experience of developing and measuring marketing campaigns had prepared me for these new challenges.

What took me the next two decades to learn on the job, in top management positions in Japan, Australia and the USA, I hope to condense here, so that your learning curve will be much shorter than mine was.

The Peter Principle

The main objective of this book is to help you overcome 'The Peter Principle'. In 1969, Dr Laurence J. Peter and Raymond Hull introduced the idea that people tend to be promoted based on their success in specific skill sets. They get promoted higher and higher until they reach a level where they can no longer excel. And there they sit, after years of high performance, in a position where they have reached what Peter and Hull somewhat comically described as their 'perfect level of incompetence'. In the marketing game, the most challenging step upwards is the step from day-to-day project management to big picture senior management. In my personal experience, this is when many previously successful marketing professionals have their competence challenged.

The lessons in this book work for all kinds of management positions. They are just as valuable for the first step from junior management to middle management as they are for later steps to senior management. They are lessons that students should study now, so that they are ready when they enter the workforce to move up the management ladder as quickly as possible. Whenever you are given responsibility for more people, more processes and/or more revenue, you have taken a big step up the management ladder and I hope this book will help lighten your load.

Chapter 1
Basic business economics
This chapter covers basic economic laws such as supply and demand. It will focus on the critical importance to any marketing programme of target segmentation and price elasticity as ways to gain more sales and/or higher prices. Marketers tend to be expert in strategies to create demand. However, without a detailed knowledge of the intricate nature of the interplay between the supply and demand curves, and the inherent strategies for maximizing profit potential along the curves, a marketer's success will be less than optimal.

Chapter 2
Vision, mission and leadership
As a manager, you must have a clear and concise vision about where you are going, and a strategy for how you are going to get there. This chapter will look at visionary companies, how they deal with balancing short-term and long-term needs, and how executives in these companies use tried and tested leadership techniques to focus both internal and external communications. When this management role is performed well, as we will see in the case of Ritz-Carlton hotels, the power of a single manager's ideas can be magnified by a shared sense of purpose with tens of thousands of employees worldwide.

Chapter 3
Competitive business strategies
Creating separation from competitors is the goal of competitive business strategy. This is how economic value is unlocked. This chapter will focus on techniques that great managers use to help create that separation, for their companies and/or their clients. Competitive business strategy starts with great research techniques. Competitive separation is only important if it adds meaningful value for your customers. It also depends on the ability to quickly and easily compare your brand to others on a number of different criteria. This can be done with a variety of simple matrices that will be discussed and demonstrated.

✕

Chapter 4
Brand identity and shareholder value

Competitive separation adds maximum value to a company or corporation when it is inextricably linked with brand identity. This chapter underlines the economic importance of nurturing brands over the long term. Branding provides special meaning and a high level of consumer emotional involvement, which drives long-term competitive advantage. Done right, individual brands can establish thought leadership for entire categories. Thought leaders are sometimes called 'lighthouse' brands because consumers can navigate the category, and view all other competitive brands, in their light. We will look at a number of different theories of branding that help managers create competitive separation that lasts for decades, not just weeks or months.

Chapter 5
Managing people

Quite simply, there is no management task as important as managing people. Everything that gets done in a company, every day, depends on the commitment and motivation of its employees. This chapter will start with a look at some basic human psychology that every manager should know. It will also explore a number of important questions that challenge managers every day, such as: 'How do I hire the best people?' and 'How do I manage political in-fighting?' The overriding themes of this chapter are the importance of culture creation and the importance of continuous communication in maintaining a positive and constructive culture.

Chapter 6
Handling a crisis

Moments of crisis are inevitable in every company. They may be the result of production issues, personnel issues, worldwide economic issues, or even corporate espionage, just to name a few. True crises are defining critical moments that test the resolve – and perhaps even the future – of the company, its managers and its culture. These are the times when managers really earn their money. This chapter will focus on the things that can be done before a crisis happens in order to be adequately prepared for it, whatever it may be. It will also discuss some simple rules that can be employed to make sure that a crisis does not spin out of control.

Chapter 7
The numbers
Marketing professionals often succeed early in their careers because they are creative thinkers. They spend a good deal of their time exploring ideas that will capture the collective imagination of their consumers. When they reach higher levels of management, they sometimes become frustrated when they realize that a significant part of their job entails financial planning, analysis and spreadsheets. Furthermore, marketing is increasingly becoming about the ability to measure the effectiveness of marketing ideas across a dizzying array of media choices, each of which throws off streams of data. This chapter gives a crash course on basic financial formulas to measure the health of your organization and simple, yet effective, techniques for measuring marketing return on investment (ROI).

Chapter 8
Ethical issues and legal compliance
Beyond the skills already highlighted, marketing managers must make sure that the work that they do with their teams meets legal guidelines and ethical practice. Ethical practice in particular is closely aligned with culture. This chapter will look at some specific ways a manager can create a more ethical and legally compliant culture.

How to get the most out of this book

>

Basics Marketing: Marketing management offers an accessible and visually engaging introduction to the study and understanding of marketing management. It also demonstrates how this knowledge can lead to the development of more effective marketing programmes. Key concepts and theories are clearly explained using real-world examples and insightful case studies. End-of-chapter discussion questions and student exercises help to further develop the concepts learned in each section.

Case studies offer insight into how the issues and ideas raised in each chapter have been addressed in the real world.

Discussion questions and exercises consolidate and contextualize the key points covered in each chapter.

Quotations help place the topic being discussed into context.

Images and captions illustrate key concepts, behaviour and campaigns.

Chapter navigation highlights the current chapter unit and lists the previous and following sections.

Running glossary provides definitions of key terms highlighted in the main text.

Box outs put the ideas discussed in the main text into a real-world context.

‹ The competitive secret weapon: research insights
Case study: Apple's iPod and iPhone
› Questions and exercises

Chapter 3 / Competitive business strategies

78 / 79

Leadership

Apple can also teach us a lot about leadership. Steve Jobs, Apple's CEO, has been the company's catalyst. His personal vision, outstanding ability to simplify complex ideas into simple thoughts and his tireless work ethic have helped to keep Apple's employees focused on innovation. From the introduction of the Macintosh in 1984 – the first home computer with a graphical user interface allowing users to interact with items on the screen – to the 2010 launch of the applications-driven iPad, Apple continues to deliver on its mission, and Jobs' vision.

How important has his personal leadership been? The company was successful and growing when he left the CEO role to start a new venture in 1985. Afterwards, its fortunes sagged, prompting his return as CEO in 1996. Since then, Apple's revenue has more than doubled, an amazing feat for a company that was already very large.

Question 1

Are there any other products or categories that you think could benefit by offering consumers a product 'system' rather than just a single product?

Question 2

How long do you think Apple's blue oceans can last before the water starts to become bloody with competition?

Question 3

What can we learn from the fact that the iPhone was inspired by computer software, which then in turn inspired the iPad computer?

> Here's to the crazy ones, the misfits,
> the rebels, the troublemakers, the
> round pegs in the square holes...
> the ones who see things differently.
>
> Apple commercial

Apple's iPad
The iPad is the latest in a series of superb strategic moves by Apple. The combination of innovative product form – a tablet computer – and embracing apps on the computing platform as well as on the mobile platform bode well for Apple's continued competitive health.

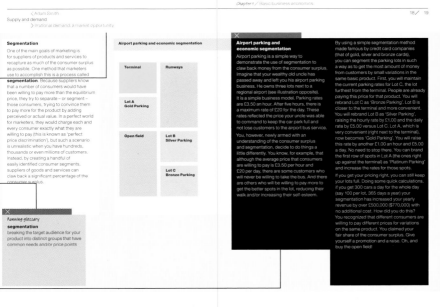

‹ Adam Smith
Supply and demand
› Irrational demand: a market opportunity

Chapter 1 / Basic business economics

18 / 19

Segmentation

One of the main goals of marketing is for suppliers of products and services to recapture as much of the consumer surplus as possible. One method that marketers use to accomplish this is a process called **segmentation**. Because suppliers know that a number of consumers would have been willing to pay more than the equilibrium price, they try to separate – or segment – those consumers, trying to convince them to pay more for the product by adding perceived or actual value. In a perfect world for marketers, they would charge each and every consumer exactly what they are willing to pay (this is known as 'perfect price discrimination'), but such a scenario is unrealistic when you have hundreds, thousands or even millions of customers. Instead, by creating a handful of easily identified consumer segments, suppliers of goods and services can claw back a significant percentage of the consumer surplus.

Airport parking and economic segmentation

Terminal	Runways
Lot A Gold Parking	
Open field	Lot B Silver Parking
	Lot C Bronze Parking

Airport parking and economic segmentation

Airport parking is a simple way to demonstrate the use of segmentation to claw back money from the consumer surplus. Imagine that your wealthy old uncle has passed away and left you his airport parking business. He owns three lots next to a regional airport (see illustration opposite). It is a simple business model. Parking rates are £3.50 an hour. After five hours, there is a maximum rate of £20 for the day. These rates reflected the price your uncle was able to command to keep the car park full and not lose customers to the airport bus service.

You, however, newly armed with an understanding of the consumer surplus and segmentation, decide to do things a little differently. You know, for example, that although the average price that consumers are willing to pay is £3.50 per hour and £20 per day, there are some customers who will never be willing to take the bus. And there are others who will be willing to pay more to get the better spots in the lot, reducing their walk and/or increasing their self-esteem.

By using a simple segmentation method made famous by credit card companies (that of gold, silver and bronze cards), you can segment the parking lots in such a way as to get the most amount of money from customers by small variations in the same basic product. First, you will maintain the current parking rates for Lot C, the lot furthest from the terminal. People are already paying this price for that product. You will rebrand Lot C as 'Bronze Parking'. Lot B is closer to the terminal and more convenient. You will rebrand Lot B as 'Silver Parking', raising the hourly rate by £1.00 and the daily rate by £5.00 versus Lot C. Lot A, which is very convenient (right next to the terminal), now becomes 'Gold Parking'. You will raise this rate by another £1.00 an hour and £5.00 a day. No need to stop there. You can brand the first row of spots in Lot A (the ones right up against the terminal) as 'Platinum Parking' and increase the rates for those spots.

If you get your pricing right, you can still keep your lots full. Doing some quick calculations, if you get 300 cars a day for the whole day (say 100 per lot, 365 days a year) your segmentation has increased your yearly revenue by over £500,000 ($770,000) with no additional cost. How did you do this? You recognized that different consumers are willing to pay different prices for variations on the same product. You claimed your fair share of the consumer surplus. Give yourself a promotion and a raise. Oh, and buy the open field!

This chapter provides a general overview of the basic principles that drive economies and competitive marketplaces. We will focus on the relationship between supply, demand and consumer utility, as well as pricing strategies based on segmentation and price elasticity. We will also look at the differences between business-to-business markets and business-to-consumer markets. The chapter closes with a case study of British Airways that ties many of these principles together.

Adam Smith was not the first economic theorist, or even the most accurate, but he was perhaps the most influential. His 1776 book, *An Inquiry into the Nature and Causes of the Wealth of Nations*, laid the foundation of modern economic thought. In it, Smith described the nature of competitive markets. On the surface, markets look somewhat turbulent, but Smith proposed that they were actually quite efficient. He envisioned markets as driven by an 'invisible hand' that guided the right amounts of goods and services just where they needed to be at just the right price.

Smith proposed that the invisible hand was, in actuality, individuals pursuing their own self-interest. The idea that men and women consistently do what is in their best interest is a cornerstone of modern economics. It is also the cornerstone of modern marketing. Therefore, it is a great place to start this book.

Is greed good?

In the 1987 movie *Wall Street*, and its 2010 sequel, actor Michael Douglas created the indelible portrait of a Wall Street insider named Gordon Gekko. Gekko uttered a line that has become one of the most famous in movie history: 'Greed… is good'. This line is interesting because it goes right to the heart of Adam Smith's observations.

So, is greed good? Economists do not make such moral judgments. What they can tell you, however, is that greed (i.e. people consistently doing what is in their own best interest) is predictable. The desire to improve one's economic status, by acquiring as many of the things that one values at the lowest cost possible, drives the vast majority of market transactions, from buying a new house to buying a box of popcorn. Marketers know this instinctively and spend a vast amount of time convincing consumers that their product offers the most value in its category.

It is not from the benevolence of the butcher, the brewer or the baker that we expect our dinner, but from their regard to their own self-interest.

Adam Smith
Philosopher
1723–1790

Gordon Gekko
Gordon Gekko, the character from the *Wall Street* movies, coined the popular and somewhat misanthropic phrase 'Greed... is good'. Despite its negative overtones, it does a good job of explaining the engine that drives economic supply and demand.

Supply and demand

The most basic tools of economics are the supply and demand curves. Simply stated, they describe the quantity of a good or service that a supplier (or producer) is willing to make available at different prices, and the quantity of a good or service that an individual (or consumer) is willing to buy at different prices. Because the producer and the consumer have different objectives (i.e. the producer wants to get the most money possible and the consumer wants to pay as little as possible) these curves go in opposite directions: the supply curve goes up and the demand curve goes down, as seen in the diagram opposite (top).

Where the supply and demand curves meet is the sweet spot where a producer's willingness to offer a certain amount of product at a certain price matches the consumer's desire to buy that amount at that price. This spot is called **equilibrium**. These two simple curves tell us a lot about how markets work in general. More importantly, they tell us how the market works for any specific product that we might be trying to sell.

Consumer surplus

An important concept related to supply and demand is the *consumer surplus*. The consumer surplus represents the amount of money that some consumers would have been willing to pay if supply of the product had been lower. It can be thought of as money that the producer has 'left on the table' for some of its consumers. Similarly, there is an equal and opposite value, *producer surplus*, which represents the amount of money that the producer would have settled for at a lower level of demand. This is the money that some consumers have 'left on the table' in the process of reaching equilibrium, as seen in the diagram opposite (bottom).

Consumer and producer surpluses
The consumer surplus is the amount of additional money some consumers would have been willing to pay at a lower level of supply – represented here by the shaded triangle above the price line (the current price) and below the demand curve (higher prices consumers would have paid). The producer surplus is the lower amount of money some suppliers would have been willing to accept at a lower level of demand – represented here by the shaded triangle below the price line (the current price) and above the supply curve (lower prices producers would have charged).

Running glossary

equilibrium
the point where consumer demand and producer supply meet each other, defining the specific price and quantity sold of a specific product

›

Supply and demand curves
Supply and demand curves
represent how many products
producers will supply at a given price
and how many products consumers
will buy at a given price.

Supply and demand curves

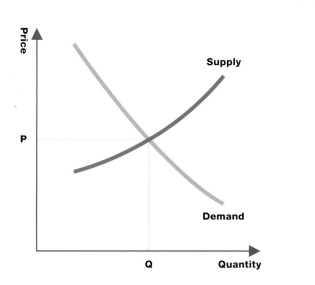

Consumer and producer surpluses

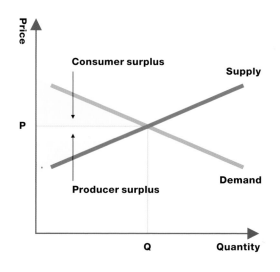

< Adam Smith
Supply and demand
> Irrational demand: a market opportunity

Segmentation

One of the main goals of marketing is for suppliers of products and services to recapture as much of the consumer surplus as possible. One method that marketers use to accomplish this is a process called **segmentation**. Because suppliers know that a number of consumers would have been willing to pay more than the equilibrium price, they try to separate – or segment – those consumers, trying to convince them to pay more for the product by adding perceived or actual value. In a perfect world for marketers, they would charge each and every consumer exactly what they are willing to pay (this is known as 'perfect price discrimination'), but such a scenario is unrealistic when you have hundreds, thousands or even millions of customers. Instead, by creating a handful of easily identified consumer segments, suppliers of goods and services can claw back a significant percentage of the consumer surplus.

Airport parking and economic segmentation

Terminal	Runways

| Lot A Gold Parking | |

| Open field | Lot B Silver Parking |

| | Lot C Bronze Parking |

Running glossary

segmentation
breaking the target audience for your product into distinct groups that have common needs and/or price points

Airport parking and economic segmentation

Airport parking is a simple way to demonstrate the use of segmentation to claw back money from the consumer surplus. Imagine that your wealthy old uncle has passed away and left you his airport parking business. He owns three lots next to a regional airport (see illustration opposite). It is a simple business model. Parking rates are £3.50 an hour. After five hours, there is a maximum rate of £20 for the day. These rates reflected the price your uncle was able to command to keep the car park full and not lose customers to the airport bus service.

You, however, newly armed with an understanding of the consumer surplus and segmentation, decide to do things a little differently. You know, for example, that although the average price that consumers are willing to pay is £3.50 per hour and £20 per day, there are some customers who will never be willing to take the bus. And there are others who will be willing to pay more to get the better spots in the lot, reducing their walk and/or increasing their self-esteem.

By using a simple segmentation method made famous by credit card companies (that of gold, silver and bronze cards), you can segment the parking lots in such a way as to get the most amount of money from customers by small variations in the same basic product. First, you will maintain the current parking rates for Lot C, the lot furthest from the terminal. People are already paying this price for that product. You will rebrand Lot C as 'Bronze Parking'. Lot B is closer to the terminal and more convenient. You will rebrand Lot B as 'Silver Parking', raising the hourly rate by £1.00 and the daily rate by £5.00 versus Lot C. Lot A, which is very convenient (right next to the terminal), now becomes 'Gold Parking'. You will raise this rate by another £1.00 an hour and £5.00 a day. No need to stop there. You can brand the first row of spots in Lot A (the ones right up against the terminal) as 'Platinum Parking' and increase the rates for those spots.

If you get your pricing right, you can still keep your lots full. Doing some quick calculations, if you get 300 cars a day for the whole day (say 100 per lot, 365 days a year) your segmentation has increased your yearly revenue by over £500,000 ($770,000) with no additional cost. How did you do this? You recognized that different consumers are willing to pay different prices for variations on the same product. You claimed your fair share of the consumer surplus. Give yourself a promotion and a raise. Oh, and buy the open field!

Irrational demand: a market opportunity

An article by Damon Darlin in *The New York Times*[1] posed the question: 'Why would anyone rush to buy a product knowing full well that it would be cheaper – and probably better – in a matter of months?' Yet that is exactly what hundreds of thousands of Apple iPad buyers did in 2010, in order to be among the first to get their hands on the hot new computing device.

As the author noted: 'Economics professors may say that such behaviour is irrational, but that does not mean that it makes no sense'. What this highlights is the existence among a number of buyers of an emotional value inherent in the product that can far outweigh its actual economic value. This tends to be especially true for the consumer segment that wants to be among the first to try or buy exciting new products. Marketers often label these consumers as 'innovators' or 'early adopters'.

Scarcity

Marketers can take advantage of this segment through high initial pricing, and also by controlling supply to maximize the sense of product scarcity. Smart marketers know that scarcity of supply for a hot product will significantly increase the price that innovators and early adopters are willing to pay. This not only brings in more money per unit sold in the short term, it also establishes a higher base price for the product when supply eventually opens up.

Wikipedia has a wonderful definition of scarcity: 'The problem of infinite human needs and wants, in a world of finite resources'. What this implies is that supply and demand are not just independent functions trying to find equilibrium. For managers of marketing, it means that well-managed supply can actually stimulate higher levels of demand.

Perhaps today's best brand at using a scarcity strategy to maximize the amount of money that a segmented group of people will pay for a product is Hermès. Their Birkin bags, named after the French actress Jane Birkin, use exotic leathers, take 48 hours to make by hand and are sold in Hermès boutiques on unpredictable schedules and in limited quantities. You might think that a bag like this would cost upwards of £1,000 ($1,600). Yet people line up for hours at just the hint of being able to attain one and regularly pay upwards of £6,500 ($10,000) for the privilege. For Hermès, scarcity is a wildly profitable strategy.

Nintendo Wii

The launch of the Nintendo Wii in 2006 was a good example of limited supply increasing consumer anticipation. When the product was launched, supply was far below demand and the situation stayed that way for a very long time. Many analysts believed that Nintendo deliberately kept supply well below demand to maintain a frenzy among consumers. Demand hit such a fever pitch that a grey market soon appeared where parents (including me!) were paying well above the retail price in order to get their kids a Wii in time for Christmas.

As one top video-game blog posting put it at the time:

'Over two months after its release, Nintendo Wii is still the hottest, and most unattainable, gaming console on the market. Being such a hot commodity, one would think that Nintendo is distributing as many Wiis as possible. This is clearly not the case, as many gamers end up leaving their 8am trips to Best Buy and other such stores empty-handed. So, this being the case, is the shortage of Wiis a good thing for Nintendo?

'The answer is YES, without a doubt. The scarcity of the Wii has helped to keep it the #1 console, topping PS3 and the earlier XBox 360. A sort of "buzz" has been created calling for everyone to take part in this revolutionary gaming experience. The shortage also keeps gamers anxious and focused on obtaining the Wii, which in turn makes it the topic of numerous conversations.' [2]

Was Nintendo playing the scarcity game? They are not admitting it, and it is more likely that production capacity drove their supply curve. But either way, there are two lessons to be learned. First, that controlling supply for hot products can heighten demand and pricing. Second, it usually only works if your product is something special. The Wii was, and is still, something very special: a unique and breakthrough gaming experience.

The first lesson of economics is scarcity.

Thomas Sowell
Writer and economist

Perhaps the most important aspect of supply and demand for marketing managers to master is an understanding of *price elasticity*. Price elasticity is about knowing how sensitive the demand for your product will be when the price for that product is increased or decreased. Conversely, it is about knowing what the correct pricing for a product should be if supply or demand for the product shifts up or down.

Elasticity depends on how steep the curves are. Marketers usually fixate on consumer demand, since for most products the supply curve is fairly standard and consistent. If the demand curve is relatively flat, it is said to be *elastic*, meaning that the consumer will react significantly to increases and decreases in price. For example, consumer demand for gum is highly elastic. If the price of gum doubles overnight, a lot fewer people will buy it. In this case, a big increase in price will almost certainly lead to far higher revenue losses than gains, as seen in the diagram opposite (top).

The price elasticity of demand is normally pronounced. In other words, sales respond noticeably to price change. An average figure for a large sample of brands is an elasticity of minus 1.8, which means that every 10% boost in price will result in an 18% sales drop.

Inelasticity

If the demand curve is relatively steep, then it is said to be *inelastic*. In other words, increases in price will lead to only a small drop in demand. For example, the demand curve for petrol and cigarettes are significantly more inelastic than gum. If petrol prices rise, people will often cut back in other areas so that they can still afford to drive to work or go to the places that they want to in their car. Similarly, hefty taxes have made cigarettes very expensive but the high prices do not deter hard-core smokers.

For products such as cigarettes and petrol, increases in price can lead to significantly more revenue gains than losses, as seen in the diagram opposite (bottom).

When demand is inelastic and supply is restricted, prices and profits can rise rapidly. However, the opposite is also true. When demand is inelastic and supply increases, prices can collapse very quickly. After all, if the supply of petrol increases there is still only so much driving anyone feels like doing. The top oil-producing countries have therefore created an oil cartel (OPEC) to avoid just such a problem by artificially limiting supply.

Elastic and inelastic demand curves

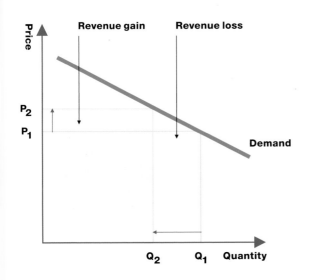

Elastic and inelastic demand curves

Elastic demand (top) means that the quantity of a good sold is very sensitive to pricing – represented here by a flatter demand line. The flatter line means that when the price of a product goes up (or down) a little, demand for the product goes up (or down) a lot.

Inelastic demand (bottom) means that the quantity sold is less sensitive to pricing – represented here by a steeper demand line. The steeper line means that when the price of a product goes up (or down) a lot, demand for the product goes up (or down) a little.

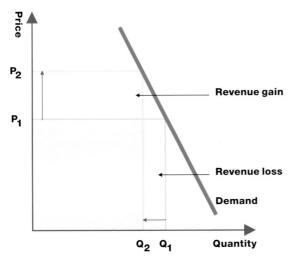

Marketing's effect on elasticity

Think about this: marketing not only affects the total amount of demand, it can reshape the elasticity of demand. John Philip Jones, professor emeritus at Syracuse University, has written numerous books on advertising and economics. In his book *How Much is Enough: Getting the Most from Your Advertising Dollar*, he presented the case of the California Avocado Advisory Board. Because consumer demand for avocados is highly inelastic (i.e. people who like avocados really like to eat them, but there are only so many avocados that anyone wants to eat), avocado growers were prone to big drops in price during any year when there was a bumper crop. As we've learned, when demand is inelastic, excess supply drives prices way down.

In response, the growers got together and developed an advertising campaign. The first result of the campaign, not surprisingly, was that it raised overall demand for avocados by raising awareness of all the different ways that you can consume them. But there was evidence that it also did something else. By introducing a new group of users who were more elastic in their demand, overall demand became more elastic.

In the world of commodity foods, where supply is often dictated by the weather, this marketing programme provided a huge benefit. In years where supply increased substantially, the avocado growers were able to better stabilize their prices.

Even when supply was limited, they were still better off because the overall rate of demand was higher, more than making up for the increased elasticity of demand.

Looking at the avocado market is instructive because it is a simple product with only indirect competition (for example, various dips and salad vegetables). Fewer competitive variables make it easier to see the effect of the advertising campaign on demand. However, the price elasticity concept is even more valuable when examining highly competitive markets, which are more typical. Jones notes: 'In these cases, a price increase leading to a loss of sales does not mean consumers stop buying in the product category, it just means they have switched to a competitive brand. In this sense, price elasticity is really a measure of substitution.'

It follows that one of the main roles of marketing is to inhibit substitution by making your brand unique in the minds of buyers. When your marketing efforts make demand for your brand more inelastic, it means that your consumers are less willing to substitute other brands for it. In a highly competitive market, unlike for commodities such as avocados, inelasticity for your product has huge a upside and very little downside.

PlayStation 3: Understanding elasticity

Understanding the elasticity of demand for products is a critical role for marketing managers. If they have a good picture of the shape of consumer demand, they will make smart pricing decisions that maximize the company's ability to gain more profit, whenever demand or the competitive situation changes. If they get it wrong, the consequences can be dire. Sony learned this lesson the hard way in 2007 when they launched the PlayStation 3. The gigantic worldwide success of the previous generation PlayStation 2 meant that they had high hopes for the launch of the new console. The PlayStation 3 was a lot better; it had some great new features, such as a Blu-ray player.

But Sony greatly misinterpreted demand for a significantly higher-priced game console. Consumers' demand was more elastic than Sony had thought it would be. As the price went sharply up, demand went sharply down. In a few short years, PlayStation's misunderstanding of consumer demand, combined with the competitive pressure of Nintendo Wii's revolutionary gaming experience, led to PlayStation going from the king of gaming consoles to an also-ran.

Movements in elasticity

The case of the California avocado growers shows how marketing can increase demand while simultaneously reshaping the elasticity of that demand. This can lead to more relative revenue, whether supply goes up or down. As seen here, the demand curve shifted to the right (i.e. overall demand increased, commanding higher prices) and it also flattened. These combined demand effects protected the avocado growers from collapsing prices in years when bumper crops flooded the market (i.e. when S1 shifts to S2).

Movements in elasticity

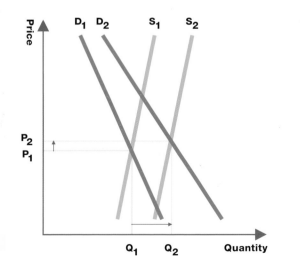

Chris Anderson, the editor-in-chief of *Wired* magazine, has been a leading thinker regarding the economics of marketing in the Internet age. In his first book, *The Long Tail*, he explained the 'long tail' economic theory whereby Internet wholesalers have an advantage in being able to stock and sell lots of low-selling items over a long period of time. Because they don't need to limit their physical stock to just hot-selling items, they are able to satisfy (and profit from) lots of previously unfilled consumer demand for slower selling items. Internet retailers have a distinct supply-side advantage over 'bricks and mortar' stores that have limited space.

In 2009, Anderson published another book entitled *Free: The Future of a Radical Price*. In it, he explained how any product built using the three computing platforms of processing power, bandwidth and digital storage will go down in price over time, and how in many cases the price will drop to nothing (and the products will be free).

Unlike physical products, such as Hermès' Birkin bag, that cultivate scarcity of supply, digital products, such as web browsers and media websites, live in a world of supply abundance.

Supply of processing power, bandwidth and digital storage is increasing at an astounding rate. Anderson pegs the net deflation rate in the online world at 50%! That means that whatever it costs to post content or stream a video today will cost half as much in a year. This is one reason that so many things on the Internet are free; costs to distribute content on the Web are halving while speed, capacity and so on are doubling.

Internet content suppliers can offer things at close to zero because they know for a certainty that their costs of distribution will be lower tomorrow. They can even offer many products at zero, or sometimes even less than zero (for example, offering people incentives to try their free online product), as long as they connect to and/or help drive profits for at least one of their revenue producing products. This is how Google works. Most Google products are completely free, such as Gmail or YouTube (YouTube is owned by Google), but they all connect to, and help drive, Google's search product, which makes lots of money through search ads. As Anderson notes: 'Google doesn't sell space. It sells users' intentions – what they've declared their interests in, in the form of a search query. And that's a scarce resource.'

> *People are making a lot of money charging nothing. Not nothing for everything, but nothing for enough that we have essentially created an economy as big as a good-sized country around the price of $0.00.*
>
> Chris Anderson
> Author of *Free: The Future of a Radical Price*

Google Maps with Street View
Google uses free services, such as its map and street view application, to draw people into their profit-making search service.

An abundance of content

For media executives, the abundant supply of online content is a huge challenge. The flood of free content has shaken the old media model to the core, especially for newspapers. Like a bumper crop of avocados, it has media companies scrambling to make money. For product marketers and advertisers, the news is better. Although some media companies will be washed away in the flood of content supply, the ones that remain will rely heavily on product advertising to make ends meet. This will offer a vast array of opportunities to finely segment audiences and to expose finer slices of the consumer surplus for those marketers smart enough to identify them.

In factories, companies are constantly looking to create **economies of scale**. What this means is that as the size (or scale) of production increases, the cost per unit produced decreases. This is because operational efficiency increases when more products are produced. This is one reason why, over time, the prices for most products fall. (Another reason is increased competition over time.) A simple way to think about this is to consider that a factory making a new automobile does not need to hire twice as many people, or to buy twice the equipment, in order to build twice as many cars as production ramps up.

As production increases, the people and the machinery will reach a higher level of efficiency (number of cars divided by labour input) before the company needs to make the decision to add more resources.

Trying to attain economies of scale is not just a factory phenomenon. It is just as true for service-based industries and disciplines, such as marketing. For a marketing manager, as your staff grows over time you should be looking to maximize their work output before adding new staff. In that way, the marketing organization becomes more efficient and contributes an increasing amount of value to your company's bottom line.

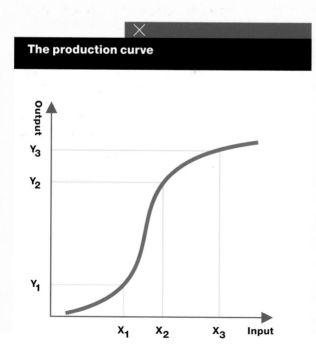

The production curve

The production curve
The production curve shows that returns to scale are uneven. As a business grows from its early stages, smaller production input (x-axis) can lead to dramatically greater output (y-axis). As seen here, the small increase from X1 to X2 leads to a large output increase from Y1 to Y2. As the organization achieves larger scale, this slows down (i.e. the curve flattens out) and can even become negative. As seen here, the increase of input from X2 to X3 is more than the resultant output from Y2 to Y3.

X

Running glossary

economies of scale
the reduction in cost per unit
produced as a result of increased
operational efficiency

Your marketing organization should aim
to create more revenue today at a lower
relative cost than it did yesterday, even when
total cost increases.

For example, if a marketing organization
succeeded in selling £1,000,000 worth of
programming at a total labour cost of
£250,000 in 2010, then growth with
economies of scale would imply that it should
be able to sell approximately £2,000,000 of
programming at a total labour cost of around
£400,000 in 2013. Costs increased 60%,
but due to economies of scale (i.e. greater
efficiency due to growth in output), revenue
grew 100%. Cost as a percentage of revenue
dropped from 25% to 20%. This is known as
increasing returns to scale.

The lesson here is simple. Successful
marketing managers know that growth
is only effective if it takes advantage of
economies of scale. Understanding this
basic economic principle can help the new
manager to develop the right goals for his or
her organization.

The theory of the low base

A corollary to economies of scale is the
theory of the low base. This refers to the fact
that the increase in operational efficiency that
should accompany growth does not occur
evenly. It is not a set percentage. In fact, it
depends on how big you are in the first place.
In other words, when you are already very big,
you may have come close to maximizing any
efficiency gains you can make by increasing
scale. Conversely, when you are small, there
are very large gains to be made by increasing
scale. When you are small and growing,
returns to scale can be dramatic. In the early
days of any small operation, small additional
inputs can lead to dramatic outputs. This is
the conundrum of scale: large scale is more
efficient than small scale, but small scale
increases in efficiency more dramatically
than large scale.

Why is this important? It tells us that as
our marketing operation grows, we should
expect more rapid efficiency growth
(i.e. increasing returns to scale) in the
early stages and less rapid efficiency growth
in the later stages. This also helps a good
manager to avoid hubris. When smaller
operations deliver incredibly high efficiency
and return on investment, managers often
think they are geniuses. The theory of the
low base tells us that these growth rates are
to be expected.

Negotiation through an economic prism
> Business-to-business versus business-to-consumer

One thing that managers do a lot of is negotiation. Sometimes these negotiations are formal, such as negotiating a contract between companies. Other times they are more informal, such as negotiating the support of a senior executive for a key budget proposal. The ability to successfully negotiate issues big and small is a hallmark of a great manager; the kind of manager who gets promoted regularly. Those who can't negotiate successfully often stagnate in their careers. As the saying goes: 'You don't get what you deserve, you get what you negotiate'.

You might wonder why the subject of negotiation is included in a chapter on basic business economics. It is because I have found that a very successful way to approach negotiation is to look at it less subjectively (i.e. less as an issue of what you want to achieve in this current negotiation) and more objectively (i.e. more as a process that consistently adheres to simple economic principles).

During a negotiation, it would be wise not to take anything personally. If you leave personalities out of it, you will be able to see opportunities more objectively.

Brian Koslow
American author and entrepreneur

Utility

To understand how to negotiate successfully, we need to think about something that economists call *utility*. Utility is the ability of something to satisfy one or more of a consumer's needs or wants. There is a whole school of economic theory devoted to utility. It is applied to such things as bilateral trade; when two people, two groups, or even two countries exchange one thing for another. It is very useful to think of any negotiation as a trade, to think less about you getting what you want and more about maximizing the utility of both parties. Good negotiation should aim to reach a point where both sides maximize their utility (i.e. each side gets the most of what they value).

Traditionally, economics viewed negotiation as a process where both parties tenaciously focused on achieving their own self-interest at every step. This adversarial process would gradually reach an optimal position where each side gave up only what they had to in order to get the most of what they wanted. In this form, negotiation is a high-stakes card game where you never let the other side see your cards.

Later, through the development of new economic ideas by, among others, John Nash (the Princeton professor and Nobel Prize-winner made famous in the movie *A Beautiful Mind*), negotiation started to be seen differently. It was increasingly clear that full knowledge of the negotiating goals and strategies of each side by the other side could actually increase the opportunity to achieve a better solution for both sides. In other words, when each side makes their decisions taking into account the needs, wants and decisions of the other side, the negotiation is more efficient and more effective at maximizing the utility of both parties.

As an economic principle, and a management lesson, this has a vital implication: the most important step in any negotiation is to find out exactly what the other side values and to tell them what you value. This is a poker game with all the cards on the table. The corollary is that if each side focuses on maximizing the other side's value, while not giving up the things that they value, the results can be extremely positive for both. This is what is called a win-win negotiation. These are the sorts of negotiations that great managers conduct again and again, both formally and informally.

Business-to-business versus business-to-consumer

Marketing is about markets. Markets are specific groups of people or organizations that buy your products. The two most basic and important types of marketing are business-to-business (B2B) marketing and business-to-consumer (B2C) marketing. The difference between the two might seem another odd addition to a chapter on economics, but there is a good reason it has been put here.

We have learned that a nuanced understanding of the economics of supply and demand is critical to successful marketing management. The difference between B2B and B2C is best looked at not as the self-evident difference between selling goods and services to consumers and businesses, but rather as two fundamentally different types of economic demand perpetuated by the same group of people.

John Favalo is managing partner of Group B2B at Eric Mower and Associates (EMA), a top B2B advertising agency in the US. He notes that a core principle of B2B is an understanding that 'the buyer is not always the user'. This is a simple distinction, but a critically important one. The people who work in businesses are the same B2C consumers who buy things for themselves every day. In a B2B context, however, these same people are buying things that others will be using. The others may simply be people in their department or company, but often they are buying things that will be part of a chain that goes from the buying company to their eventual consumers.

Favalo uses the example of the lighting in a room. In any room you happen to be in, the lighting is part of a chain of demand that goes from the architect of the building to the contractor to the contracting supply company to the company that made the original lights. Someone at every stage made the decision to buy the lighting system based on someone else's needs.

The lesson for marketing managers is that B2B customers are buying for fundamentally different reasons than B2C customers (i.e. their demand curves and elasticities for the exact same product will be different in these different contexts). Additionally, marketers need to understand not just the demand of the initial buyer, but also the entire chain of demand, down to the eventual consumer.

Successful business-to-business marketing

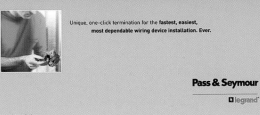

PlugTail: Reaching electricians

One of EMA's clients is Legrand/Pass & Seymour, one of the world's leading suppliers of electrical wiring devices. They have developed an intricate understanding of the day-to-day challenges that electricians face. Recently, they launched their new PlugTail™ product, a unique connector that cuts the time it takes an electrician to install an electrical wiring device by 50%. The electrician doing the job is rarely the one purchasing the equipment, so EMA's marketing campaign convinces the project managers, or their purchasing agents, that their device would make the site electrician's job much easier. Better yet, PlugTail's easier installation means that contractors can use less-skilled labour to install them, freeing up experienced electricians to perform higher level tasks. Contractors are happy. Purchasers are happy. Electricians are happy. This is B2B marketing at its best.

Case study: British Airways – branding business class

We learned in this chapter that smart marketing managers understand the importance of unlocking profit from the consumer surplus. They do this by taking the same basic product and segmenting it in a way that different consumers will pay different amounts of money for it. Earlier, we mentioned credit card companies as a good example of this approach.

Another good example is airlines. Although every seat on the plane is going to the same place, by adding certain benefits (e.g. a bigger seat, faster check-in, better food), the cost differential for a seat can be dramatic. Looking at recent flights from London to New York, it is common for an economy seat to cost around £500 ($800), for a business-class seat on the same flight to cost five times that (or £2,500/$4,000), and for a first class seat to cost almost eight times the economy fare (or £4,000/$6,400). That's a lot of extra money (and profit) for better food and a bigger seat.

One of the first airlines to master segmentation in the airline industry was British Airways. They did it by not only creating a business-class product, but by masterfully branding it and emphasizing its emotional benefits as well as its physical ones. Unlike other airlines, who just called their products 'business class', British Airways dubbed their's 'Club World'. They evoked an image of being in a private club, a cocoon of pampering service in the company of other club members.

In one of their earliest commercials for the product, in the late 1980s, they showed a businessman travelling from New York to London on the overnight 'red eye' flight for a big meeting the next morning. His competitors in London are gleefully anticipating how tired and hungry he will be because the company won't allow first-class travel. As they put it, he will be 'like a lamb to the slaughter' in the meeting. Of course, he arrives refreshed and ready to win; his competitors are justifiably distraught.

What British Airways did was to create a unique competitive position for their business-class product. They gave it a name and an image that was unique in the market. Most importantly, they understood that segmentation is not just a tactical business strategy: it is a penetrating look into the psyche of airline passengers. Buying seats that are five or eight times more expensive for a seven-hour flight is not just about more comfort. Sometimes it is about ego: being treated like a club member. Sometimes it is about job performance: a few thousand dollars can pale in comparison to doing a bad business deal because you are not on top of your game.

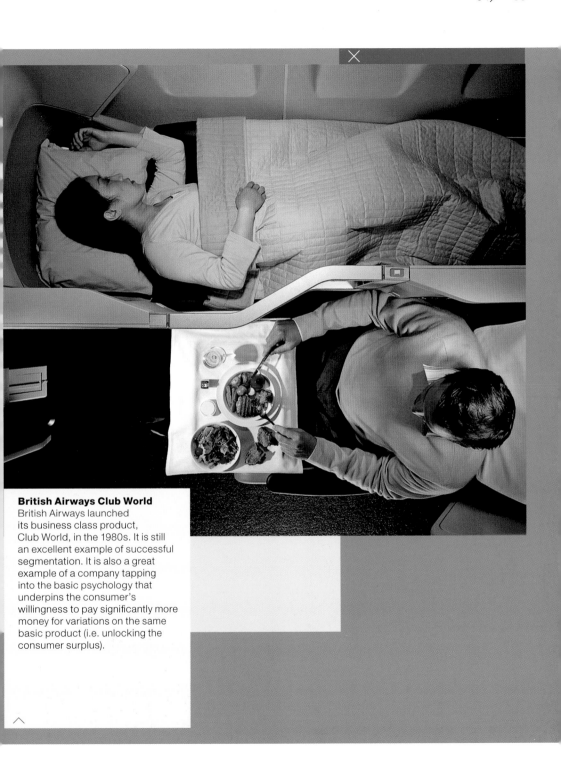

British Airways Club World
British Airways launched
its business class product,
Club World, in the 1980s. It is still
an excellent example of successful
segmentation. It is also a great
example of a company tapping
into the basic psychology that
underpins the consumer's
willingness to pay significantly more
money for variations on the same
basic product (i.e. unlocking the
consumer surplus).

〈 Business-to-business versus business-to-consumer
Case study: British Airways – branding business class
〉 Questions and exercises

Consumer psychology

Still today, few airlines understand consumer psychology as well as British Airways. Most airlines, for example, still label their business-class product as nothing more than 'business' or 'business class'. After the success of Club World, British Airways extended their thinking to their economy product, renaming it 'World Traveller'. They have even created a new segmentation called 'World Traveller Plus', which offers economy seats with more legroom at a price point above economy class, but well below business class.

Considering that a vast majority of passengers travel economy class – as do many business-class travellers when they are travelling on their own money – do you think customers react better to a product whose name focuses on how little they want to pay, or on the fact that they aspire to travel the world? The answer is simple, but the thinking that gets you there is not. British Airways and their marketing team understand the consumer psychology and economic possibilities that lie behind successful segmentation. They have created a product and positioning for its business class that has been the envy of the industry for years.

Limitations

British Airways is also a cautionary tale about the limits of great marketing. While great marketing can stimulate demand and maximize profits, it cannot always overcome larger economic, environmental or operational issues. British Airways' revenue has been battered in recent years by factors such as the spike in oil prices in 2008, the worldwide financial crisis in 2009 and service interruptions due to the eruption of a volcano in Iceland in 2010. These challenges were combined with British Airways' huge pension debt and a walkout by service staff over the airline's plans to cut back staff and freeze wages. These are the types of issues that challenge leadership to have a strong vision and mission to get their companies through rocky times, which is the focus of our next chapter.

British Airways' challenges
In April 2010, the impressively named Eyjafjallajökull volcano erupted in Iceland. The resultant ash caused service interruptions across Europe. According to the International Air Transport Association (IATA), the disruption cost the airline industry more than $1.7 billion in lost revenues. In times of trouble, a strong vision, mission and leadership are essential.

Question 1
Can you think of any further customer segmentation or differentiating pricing ideas for airlines?

Question 2
What do you think the price difference between economy and business airfares says about the elasticity of demand for business-class travel?

Question 3
Do you think it is smarter to price World Traveller Plus closer to the price of a business class seat or an economy seat? Why?

Questions and exercises

>

Discussion questions

1

When is it good for the economy for people to pursue their own self-interest? When is it bad?

2

Which type of product do you think generally creates a larger consumer surplus; a high-priced luxury product such as cosmetics, a daily staple product like paper towels, or a commodity such as oranges?

3

Which type of purchase do you think is more likely to be an impulse purchase, a consumer product or a B2B product?

Exercises

1

In teams, try to create a segmentation strategy for Harley Davidson. How would you unlock the consumer surplus in the motorcycle industry? Compare similarities and differences in the teams' approaches.

2

Imagine that you are the marketing director of a fast food company. How might your communications to consumers who visit your stores (B2C) be different from your communications to companies you are trying to convince to put your products in their chain of cafeterias (B2B)?

3

Brainstorm concepts for a new online shopping product to compete with Amazon. How would the site make money? What aspects would be completely free? What aspects would be advertising supported? What aspects would you charge users for directly?

Suggested further reading

Anderson, C. (2007) *The Long Tail: How Endless Choice is Creating Unlimited Demand.* (New York: Hyperion)

Anderson, C. (2009) *Free: The Future of a Radical Price.* (New York: Hyperion)

Jones, J.P. (1992) *How Much is Enough: Getting the Most from Your Advertising Dollar.* (New York: John Wiley & Sons)

Jones, J. P. (2002) *The Ultimate Secrets of Advertising.* (California: Sage Publications, Inc.)

Nellis, J.G. and D. Parker (2006) *Principles of Business Economics (2nd Ed).* (New Jersey: Prentice Hall)

Summary

The primary goal of most marketing is to sell products or services in order to make profit. Managers need a working knowledge of the interplay between supply and demand in order to maximize those profits. Beyond supply and demand, successful managers often look at a variety of management functions, such as negotiation, through an economic lens.

This chapter focuses on management and the big picture. It is about management as leadership. Great leaders set a course that others follow with enthusiasm. They follow not because they have to – because the boss said so – but rather because they earnestly believe that the vision laid out by management is a good one.

Over the following pages, we will focus on the process of turning an inspirational dream into simple vision and mission statements that can be shared with the whole organization. We will also look at the habits of some consistently visionary companies, such as Ritz-Carlton. Finally, we will consider some specific suggestions for improving management leadership in one of the most critical areas for the 21st century and beyond: sustainability.

If something can be said to be the primary role of management, it is to have a strong vision of success and to inspire everyone in the company to achieve it. Some companies, such as Apple Computer, have visionary leaders like Steve Jobs who consistently point the company towards the future. Other companies use a painstaking process of information gathering and management discussion to chart their course. Either model can be successful.

At Saatchi & Saatchi, the worldwide advertising agency where I worked, the process of creating a vision was an inclusive and iterative process that helped to create buy-in from key managers around the globe because they had been involved. Importantly, our CEO Kevin Roberts did not call it our vision; he called it our 'inspirational dream'. This was a reminder that having a vision is only half of the equation; it must also inspire people to achieve it.
Inspiration comes from engaging human emotions. Saatchi & Saatchi's inspirational dream is: 'To be revered as a hothouse for world-changing creative ideas.'

Stretch goals

In the early 1960s, US President John F. Kennedy presented just such a vision in a speech at Rice University in Texas. He stated the goal for the US space programme: 'We choose to go to the moon in this decade…' It was a simple, powerful and audacious statement for a space programme that was considerably behind the Russian programme, and which was nowhere near having the capability to put a man on the moon.

What Kennedy's speech shows us is that great visions are not easy to achieve. They are stretch goals. Stretch goals are important because they bring out the best in people; they inspire harder work and greater achievement. As Kennedy put it, the US was going to do the things necessary to go to the moon '…not because they are easy, but because they are hard; because that goal will serve to organize and measure the best of our energies and skills.' For the same reason, Saatchi & Saatchi pairs its inspirational dream with a statement of its 'greatest imaginable challenge', which is to be named 'agency of the year' in every market in which they operate.

When creating a vision, the focus should be on simplicity (it should be easy for people to understand), emotional engagement (it should be inspiring to employees), and challenge (it should be a stretch to achieve).

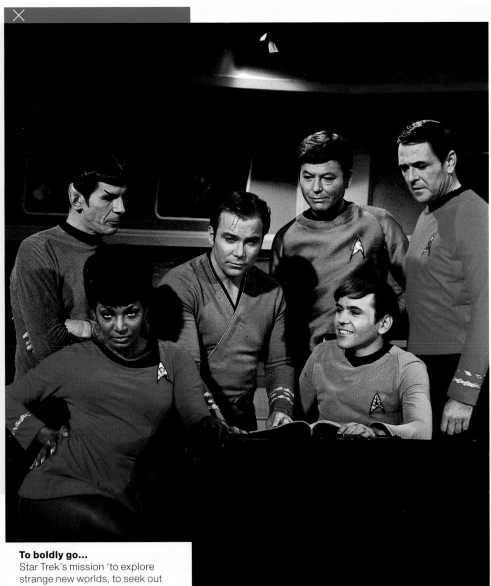

To boldly go...
Star Trek's mission 'to explore
strange new worlds, to seek out
new life and new civilizations,
to boldly go where no man has
gone before' is a clear, succinct
statement of intent. What is good for
Star Trek is good in the boardroom.
Companies do well when they have
clear, inspiring and challenging
mission statements.

< Inspirational dreams
Vision and mission statements
> Habits of visionary companies

Most companies create some sort of vision or mission statement. Alternatively, some prefer to just state their unique philosophy. Vision focuses on 'where we are going'. Mission focuses on 'how we are going to get there'. Philosophy focuses on 'what makes our company unique'. Some companies combine all three in one statement.

Vision and mission statements are best when they are short. Long-winded statements are often used to cover up the lack of something important to say. Nike is a great example of a company with a short, powerful mission statement:

'To bring inspiration and innovation to every athlete in the world.'

Combined with the brand's rallying cry, 'Just Do It', Nike has been able to inspire employees and athletes alike. The result has been a dominant position in the athletic shoe and apparel market over a period of decades.

Capital isn't scarce; vision is.

Sam Walton
Executive and founder of
Wal-Mart Stores Inc.

Big hairy audacious goals (BHAGs)

In their seminal business book, *Built to Last*, Jim Collins and Jerry Porras underscored the importance of vision and mission statements encapsulating challenging stretch goals. As they put it, they should go beyond 'verbose, meaningless, impossible-to-remember' statements. Rather, they should articulate 'big hairy audacious goals' or 'BHAGs'. They point to the powerful example of General Electric in the 1990s and compare it to their closest competitor at the time, Westinghouse. General Electric's Chairman and CEO at the time, Jack Welch, presented a powerful BHAG to his company:

'Become #1 or #2 in every market we serve and revolutionize this company to have the speed and agility of a small enterprise.'

Westinghouse, on the other hand, created a vision statement that was, on the surface, about leadership, but that is far less specific and inspiring:

'Total quality. Market leadership. Technology driven. Global. Focused growth. Diversified.'

Since then, General Electric's growth has far out-performed Westinghouse's.

Vision and mission statements can be powerful management tools. At their best, they are simple and unique and can inspire employees to do remarkable things that put their companies far ahead of the competition. At their worst, they are hackneyed phrases that offer little differentiation and no genuine inspiration.

Harrods and Lexus

Two of my personal favourite mission statements are those of Harrods and Lexus. Harrods, the iconic London department store, has a wonderfully aspirational mission statement:

'To be the number one department store in the world for luxury branded merchandise.... Through a combination of product, innovation and eccentricity, we aim to provide every customer with a truly unforgettable experience in our quintessentially British environment.'

Although this statement could be shorter (and I've already shortened it), it has the hallmarks of a great BHAG. Will every customer have an unforgettable experience? It is unlikely. Yet, a company whose employees are intent on making every customer's experience unforgettable will undoubtedly create something very special. How special? Harrods was sold in May 2010 for £1.5 billion ($2.24 billion)!

In the late 1980s, Toyota, which at that time was known for small, high-quality, fuel-efficient cars, launched a new full-sized luxury sedan in the United States. It was named Lexus and was targeted to directly compete with the market leaders – Cadillac, Mercedes and BMW. The entire strategy was audacious. Lexus enshrined their vision and mission for the new brand in a document that carried – and which still carries today – almost biblical importance within the company. Aptly, it was called 'the Lexus covenant'. Lexus employees did not just read the covenant; they had to sign it. This is the Lexus covenant:

'Lexus will enter the most competitive, prestigious automobile race in the world. Over 50 years of Toyota automotive experience has culminated in the creation of Lexus cars. They will be the finest ever built.

'Lexus will win the race because: Lexus will do it right from the start. Lexus will have the finest dealer network in the industry. Lexus will treat each customer as we would a guest in our home.

'If you think you can't, you won't.... If you think you can, you will! We can, we will.'

When Lexus launched in the US, they did indeed deliver great cars and a dealership experience that was second to none. Within a few years, Lexus was the number one luxury import in the US. Within a decade, it was the number one luxury car overall, a position it has continued to hold.

Vision and mission statements can only do so much. They can provide inspiration and impetus, but they need to be supported by strong corporate cultures too. In *Built to Last*, Collins and Porras also looked at the cultures of highly successful companies. They noted that many of these companies had almost cult-like cultures. They also had some common traits, or habits, that were telltale signs of visionary companies. Let's take a look at three of the most important of these 'habits'.

'Try a lot of stuff and keep what works'

Great companies are religious about maintaining dominance in their core business, but they also constantly experiment with lots of new, sometimes seemingly crazy, product ideas. The authors labelled this idea 'branching and pruning'. Like a tree, new business ideas branch off, and in order to keep the tree healthy, weak branches are trimmed, while strong branches are encouraged to grow. Companies like 3M, American Express and Johnson & Johnson were cited as organizations that often stumbled into great new ideas (such as Scotch Tape) which allowed them to evolve and grow. Without this sort of growth, through a culture that combines corporate **skunk works**, playfulness and serendipity, even the most successful companies can stagnate and lose their edge over time.

More recently, the importance of serendipitous experimentation has been brought into sharp focus by Nassim Nicholas Taleb in his influential book *The Black Swan*. The book focuses on the huge importance and impact of improbable and unforeseen events. Taleb states: 'The reason free markets work is because they allow people to be lucky, thanks to aggressive trial and error…'

Running glossary

skunk works
a small group of people who work on a project in an unconventional way

Post-it notes: new product serendipity

While a worker at 3M's research labs was trying to develop a strong adhesive, he inadvertently developed a very weak adhesive instead. Many years later, another 3M worker had trouble keeping his place in a church hymnal (the papers he stuck in to hold his place kept falling out). He remembered the weak adhesive and put some on small pieces of paper making them easy to stick and remove. Thus, one of 3M's most popular products, Post-it notes, was born, or rather stumbled upon.

Indeed, as the former CEO of 3M Corporation, Richard Carlton, points out: 'Our company has, indeed, stumbled onto some of its new products. But never forget that you can only stumble if you are moving.'

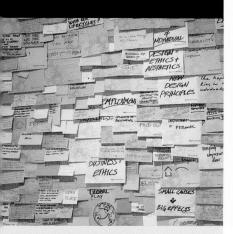

A serendipitous invention

'Home-grown management'

Because culture within corporations is so important, many visionary companies place a premium on promoting from within their own ranks, rather than hiring from outside. This is not to say that it doesn't make sense, on occasion, to bring in outsiders who can provide a new set of skills or a new perspective. But it does mean that if your culture and vision are consistently able to provide inspiration and results, it is best not to dilute it too much. Earlier, we mentioned Jack Welch of General Electric, as noted in *Built to Last,* by Collins and Porras: 'To have a Welch-calibre CEO is impressive. To have a century of Welch-calibre CEOs all grown from the inside – well, that is one key reason why GE is a visionary company.'

'Good enough never is'

Great managers instil a feeling in their staff that there is always another hill to climb. They create organizations that see success not as an end result, but rather as an opportunity to tackle the next challenge. Some of the best companies enshrine this philosophy with the words *continuous improvement*. In Japanese companies, for example, it is called *kaizen*. In such organizations, any discussion of maintaining the status quo is anathema. They create specific mechanisms to avoid complacency. In the case of the giant retailer Wal-Mart, the founder Sam Walton instituted 'beat yesterday' ledgers, which tracked sales on a daily basis versus the exact same day of the week a year earlier.

< Vision and mission statements
Habits of visionary companies
> The mother of all problems

Nelson Mandela
A truly great leader will often
either be charismatic, prescient or
have the ability to stick to strong
principles that guide their decisions
and relationships. A remarkable
few combine all these qualities.

Good business leaders create a vision,
articulate the vision, passionately own
the vision, and relentlessly drive it
to competition.

Jack Welch
CEO
General Electric

Leadership secrets

When we talk about visionary habits, we are talking about more than mere management. We are talking about leadership. Leaders are often blessed with great charisma (e.g. John F. Kennedy) or great prescience (e.g. Steve Jobs). But many leaders are blessed with neither of these. In fact, some of the most successful corporate leaders could be described as boring! What they do have, which makes up for their lack of charisma or foresight, is adherence to some basic principles that make people want to follow them. Let's take a look at some of those principles:

Show integrity

They say what they mean and mean what they say. They are consistent in their interpretation of their company's values and they are consistent in presenting their own values. Because they are believed to have integrity, they are seen as credible and fair, even when they make unpopular decisions.

KISS

KISS is an acronym for 'Keep It Simple, Stupid'. Visionary leaders are relentless about boiling down complex issues into simple judgments. They make sure to frame objectives and strategies in clear, concise language, with as little hyperbole as possible, to make sure that everyone understands the challenges and can get on the same page.

Ask great questions

Bad managers jump to conclusions and often have an overwhelming desire to solve problems as quickly as possible. They prefer to make pronouncements. Leaders, on the other hand, ask open-ended questions. This allows them to deeply explore what the problem or opportunity really is. It also allows employees to examine the evidence, so that they can be part of solving the problem. When employees have been part of solving the problem, they are already bought into implementing the solution.

These leadership secrets are not so secret, but it takes a disciplined manager to stick to them consistently.

Microsoft has published a number of books on leadership under the banner 'Microsoft Executive Leadership Series'. One of these books, authored by Don Peppers and Martha Rogers, highlights the 'crisis of **short-termism**' as a major leadership challenge. Visionary leaders, by definition, are focused on the long term. However, long-term investments can be very hard to accomplish when you are up against urgent short-term demands, such as delivering increased quarterly profits. The need to drive profit today often precludes investments in the future. This common dilemma is described by Peppers and Rogers as the 'mother of all business problems'.

True measures of success

The mother of all problems has a simple, practical solution: managers need to shift their focus from false measures of success to true ones. Quarterly profits can tell you how much money you are making today, but they are poor indicators (often very poor) of the actual health of a business. A better measure of success is *trust*. Peppers' and Rogers' rationale for this is based on two simple principles:

1

'Customers will do business with you tomorrow only if they (and their friends) trust you today. Therefore, consumer trust is a prerequisite for long-term business success.'

2

'Your employees will work to earn customer trust only if they trust you, their employer. So your job is to;

a

motivate your employees to treat customers fairly and;

b

enable them to do so by providing the right tools, training, and authority for taking action.'

This success formula is simple and intuitive. We somehow know it is right on face value. But it takes great leadership and courage to shift our focus from the exigencies of quarterly reports to the core of our long-term success. Leaders need to be brave enough to follow their own good judgment and inspire their employees to trust theirs.

A great example of this kind of trust comes from the high-end US retailer Nordstrom. Their employee rule book has only one rule: 'Use your good judgment in all situations. There will be no additional rules.' High levels of trust lead to high levels of profit over time. Investing management focus to build trust may be worth a bad financial quarter.

Sustainability

Although short-termism may be the mother of all challenges, it pales in comparison to the great challenges faced by our civilization. Global warming, dwindling energy resources, air pollution and lack of clean water are just a few of the daunting challenges facing humankind.

Companies and their leaders share in the responsibility to help solve these problems. One obvious reason for this is that companies are directly responsible for many of them – one need only look at the 2010 BP oil spill in the Gulf of Mexico to see that. Another, perhaps less obvious, reason is that in order for a manager to be truly successful, they must ensure the long-term viability of their companies. Ultimately, corporate leaders must recognize that, when developing strategies, **sustainability** is a core management responsibility. Many of today's top companies are putting sustainability at the top of their management agendas. For example: Anheuser-Busch is committed to using renewable energy to brew five billion beers a year; furniture maker Herman Miller, Inc. has reduced its waste and overall emissions by over 80% and water usage by over 65%.

Running glossary

short-termism
an excessive focus on short-term results at the expense of long-term interests

sustainability
harvesting or using a resource so that the resource is not depleted or permanently damaged

⟨ Habits of visionary companies
The mother of all problems
⟩ Case study: Ritz-Carlton – inspiring leadership

Werbach's three steps to sustainability

This chapter is about vision and leadership. There is no area where corporate leadership is more necessary than in the area of sustainability. This is one area where, if we fail as managers, we fail humankind.

One of the leading thinkers on the subject of how businesses can improve their sustainability strategies is Adam Werbach, global CEO of Saatchi & Saatchi S. He has twice been elected to the worldwide board of Greenpeace and he was the youngest-ever president of the oldest environmental organization in the US, the Sierra Club. In his book, *Strategy for Sustainability*, Werbach provides practical tools for corporate leaders to start making headway against increasingly difficult sustainability challenges.

Werbach's most basic suggestion is for companies to establish an overriding sustainability goal. He suggests that taking the goal and turning it into successful action requires three key steps, as outlined below:

The corporate sector has the incentives, operational know-how, scalability and ingenuity to respond to the global challenges we face today....

Adam Werbach
Author
Strategy for Sustainability

Increase information transparency

Your company's sustainability challenges are not bad news to be kept secret or managed through a public relations programme. They are challenges that need to be shared. Transparency allows thousands of minds to offer solutions and it creates trust. Open up!

Engage employees

Employees are the people who actually make things happen in companies. They see inefficiency, waste and non-sustainable work processes more clearly than management because they interact with them on a day-to-day basis. Once engaged, they can help to identify and solve problems. Importantly, it is only by getting employees deeply involved that sustainability goes from being a management strategy to a daily reality. According to Gary Hirshberg, head of Stonyfield Farm, an organic dairy products firm:

'I think we all have to remember that all change starts at the edges. But it only becomes permanent when it makes it to the middle... [when] these new practices become widely adopted by managers and employees and are a normal part of "business as usual".'

To underscore its commitment to its corporate sustainability goals, Wal-Mart invites employees to join its *Personal Sustainability Project*, committing to small personal acts of sustainability (e.g. turning off the water when they brush their teeth, biking to work once a week, changing from fluorescent to more efficient light bulbs at home). When you combine over 1.5 million employees with small sustainable acts over a long period of time, as Wal-Mart does, the impact can be huge. Just as importantly, it raises employee consciousness of sustainable practices on the job.

Engage the network

Companies do not end with their employees. They have many stakeholders, including partner companies, suppliers, vendors and, most importantly, customers. All of these stakeholders can be inspired to help to achieve and even define your sustainability strategies. For example, Stonyfield Farm learned from one of their business partners, UPS shipping, that if their yogurt drivers made fewer left-hand turns during delivery routes, it would save a significant amount of the energy wasted waiting at lights.

Case study: Ritz-Carlton – inspiring leadership

The Credo

One company renowned for its commitment to its mission and for inspiring leadership is The Ritz-Carlton Hotel Company. Ritz-Carlton's focus is articulated as 'The Credo':

'The Ritz-Carlton Hotel is a place where the genuine care and comfort of our guests is our highest mission.

'We pledge to provide the finest personal service and facilities for our guests who will always enjoy a warm, relaxed, yet refined ambience.

'The Ritz-Carlton experience enlivens the senses, instils well-being, and fulfils even the unexpressed wishes and needs of our guests.'

Engage and empower

Ritz-Carlton's ability to deliver on this credo is legendary. They are able to do it because they consistently engage and empower their employees. One way they do it is by convening every one of their 35,000 employees worldwide, every day, for a 15-minute meeting, known as the 'line-up'. In this meeting, they review guest experiences, discuss guest issues and celebrate great feats of service by telling a 'wow story' about how one of their staff did something amazing to make a guest's stay special.

The ladies and gentlemen of The Ritz-Carlton are deeply committed to serving the disadvantaged in our communities. We partner with community organizations and social enterprises to provide aid to those in need. Our initiatives impact an array of community needs, from cooking and serving meals at homeless shelters, renovating critical community facilities, building homes and partnering on programs designed to help break the cycle of poverty.

Community footprints
The Ritz-Carlton

A typical 'wow story' comes from the Ritz-Carlton in Bali. A family had brought with them specialized eggs and milk due to their son's food allergies. Unfortunately, the milk had soured and the eggs had broken in transit. The Ritz-Carlton staff searched the town but could not find the right milk and eggs to replace them. The executive chef, however, remembered a store in Singapore that sold them. He contacted his mother-in-law, who bought the products and had them flown to Bali at no cost to the guests.[1] Now that *is* service! Or, in Ritz-Carlton parlance, it is fulfilling the unexpressed needs of their guests.

Great companies harness the power of storytelling to bring their visions to life for their employees. The wow stories told by Ritz-Carlton employees day after day bring the words of the mission into sharp focus. They spark new ideas for service, and create a sense of palpable success and pride that cold, hard words on a page never could. They are motivational because they are real.

The reputation that Ritz-Carlton has garnered for leadership is so great that other companies regularly pay to attend classes in their Leadership Centre. They offer courses in everything from anticipating customer needs (called 'Antenna Up!'), on-boarding new employees, and, not surprisingly, leadership. Their leadership also extends to community service, with courses such as 'Adding Value Through Social Responsibility'.

Inspirational leadership

Ritz-Carlton's success can be attributed in large part to the leadership of one man, Horst Schulze, who was the founding president and chief operating officer of the Ritz-Carlton Hotel Company, L.L.C. This highly charismatic leader was instrumental in defining and communicating the hotel company's operating and service standards.

As a measure of Schulze's leadership, the company won an unprecedented two National Quality Awards for service excellence under his guidance. It has been continuously voted 'best hotel company in the world' by many trade publications. Schulze himself was named 'corporate hotelier of the world' by *HOTELS Magazine*. He was also awarded the prestigious Ishikawa Medal for personal contributions to the quality movement. In 2002, he received the Hotel Sales and Marketing Association's 'International Lifetime Achievement Award'.

⟨ The mother of all problems
Case study: Ritz-Carlton – inspiring leadership
⟩ Questions and exercises

Trust

Great leaders have followers. And when followers have been led well they can be trusted to deliver. Ritz-Carlton gives an incredible amount of latitude to their employees in dealing with customers. According to the company's current president, and Schulze's successor, Simon Cooper: 'We entrust every single Ritz-Carlton staff member, without approval from their general manager, to spend up to $2,000 [£1,250] on a guest. And that's not per year. It's per incident. …this isn't just about rebating a movie because your room was late… it displays a deep trust in our staff's judgment.'[2]

A key lesson from this chapter is that management leadership is in essence about *trust*. Trust needs to be mutual, between management and employees, between brands and their customers, and between companies and society. Ritz-Carlton exemplifies a company that builds that kind of trust.

The future

Like British Airways in the previous chapter, Ritz-Carlton's journey has not always been smooth. In the 1990s, it had its share of financial issues and money-losing hotels.

However, the power of the brand, the quality of its leadership and the dedication of its employees was attractive enough for Marriott Corporation to invest over £313 million ($500 million) to purchase the company. Ritz-Carlton's single-minded focus on its mission to provide a unique guest experience, combined with Marriott's deep pockets and impressive operational skills and tools, have proved a potent combination over the last decade. Ritz-Carlton is growing and opening new hotels around the world. Its future is very bright.

We are ladies and gentlemen serving ladies and gentlemen.

Ritz-Carlton motto

Ritz-Carlton Hotel, Doha, Qatar
Ritz-Carlton staff pride themselves
on their attention to detail as part
of a company that uses a strong
mission, daily employee line-ups,
the power of storytelling and
consistent leadership training to
maintain its market-leading position.

Question 1
If you were a competitor to
Ritz-Carlton, how might you create
a different, yet equally compelling,
mission?

Question 2
If your company manufactured cars,
what kind of 'wow stories' might
inspire and motivate your employees?

Question 3
Do you think the idea of a daily
'line-up' would work for any company
or is it particularly well-suited to a
hotel company?

Discussion questions

1
Take a look at John F. Kennedy's 'moon speech' on YouTube. How important is the messenger relative to the message? What does this mean for company CEOs?

2
If you were starting a new business, how much resource would you devote to planning versus experimentation?

3
Are there times when a complicated message can actually be more effective than a simple one? When?

Exercises

1
Facebook is a dominant brand in social networking. Assume that you need to create a new brand to compete with it. Write a vision statement and a mission statement that will help you to compete with and ultimately overtake them.

2
Research Facebook's launch of their Beacon product in 2007. Debate whether the furore around privacy concerns has impacted on their long-term trust versus their short-term profits.

3
Break into teams. Pick three companies and compete to see which team can come up with the most interesting ideas on how those companies, and their employees, could improve their sustainability.

Summary

In order for a manager to be great, they need to be a leader. Leaders by definition have followers. Leadership is not just something you do; it is something that is bestowed upon you by those you lead. Leadership, at its core, is about setting a course that others are willing to follow. Great leaders have a way of articulating their vision and their team's mission in a way that is simple and imaginative.

Suggested further reading

Collins, J. C. and J. I.Porras. (1996) *Built to Last: Successful Habits of Visionary Companies*. (United Kingdom: Random House)

Peppers, D. and M. Rogers. (2008) *Rules to Break and Laws to Follow: How Your Business Can Beat the Crisis of Short-Termism*. (New Jersey: John Wiley & Sons, Inc.)

Michelli, J. A. (2008) *The New Gold Standard: Five Leadership Principles for Creating a Legendary Customer Experience Courtesy of The Ritz-Carlton Hotel Company*. (New York: McGraw Hill)

Talib, N. N. (2007) *The Black Swan: The Impact of The Highly Improbable*. (London: Allen Lane)

Werbach, A. (2009) *Strategy for Sustainability: A Business Manifesto*. (Boston: Harvard Business Press)

This chapter focuses on strategy. It defines what strategy is and is not. It looks at a variety of helpful theories about developing strategy in order to create competitive separation and advantage. We will look at a variety of simple tools that allow business people to hone in on the factors that are strategically important. Many of these tools take the form of a matrix or grid. We will discuss why this specific format is so useful.

Core to any strategic plan is a keen understanding of your target customer. We will look at some research fundamentals that help to tease out customer insights. The chapter ends with a close look at Apple and the key strategic decisions that helped to propel both the iPod and iPhone to competitive dominance.

Before developing a strategic plan, it helps to have a working definition of strategy. Most dictionaries will describe strategy as 'a plan of action'. Unfortunately, that definition can be counter productive in the rough and tumble of business management. This is because complex organizations, with dozens of managers and hundreds of employees, often aggregate their best ideas into long and complex plans of action. This is a process that I like to call 'list making'.

These plans come out of management meetings where managers list every possible idea that can help them to achieve their objectives. The problem with list making is that it defies the KISS (keep it simple, stupid) principle discussed in the last chapter. It leads to a list of actions so long that they often cannot be remembered, much less achieved. It also does not respect the fact that companies have limited resources. It dilutes precious resources over too many projects, as opposed to concentrating them on a few important ones.

Perhaps a preferable definition is: 'strategy is about making choices.' This definition underscores strategy as a process of rigorous prioritization and selection. It means that what you choose *not* to do is just as important (often more important) than what you choose to do. Everything that you choose *not* to do frees up resources and clarifies the meaning of the things that you *do* decide to do.

Competitive advantage: the hedgehog concept

In the best-seller, *Good to Great*, the author Jim Collins uses an Aesop fable that pits a fox against a hedgehog as an analogy for competitive advantage. The fox is a crafty creature with numerous strategies for catching the hedgehog. The hedgehog has a single strategy, to curl up in a spiky ball to become impervious to attack.

As Collins explains: 'Foxes pursue many ends at the same time and see the world in all its complexity…. Hedgehogs, on the other hand, simplify a complex world into a single organizing idea, a basic principle or concept that unifies and guides everything.'

When the fox and the hedgehog meet, the hedgehog always wins.

Every company would like to be the best at something, but few actually understand – with piercing insight and egoless clarity – what they actually have the potential to be the best at and, just as important, what they cannot be the best at.

Jim Collins
Good to Great

So how can companies learn to be more like hedgehogs? Collins suggests that there are three questions that every company should ask.

1
What is your company deeply passionate about?
This is not about competence; it is about passion. It is about what you love to do. When you and your employees are passionate, you are usually at your best. For example, Gillette, the razor company, just could not get passionate about the cheap, disposable razor market, so they focused their resources on sophisticated, high-end, and high-priced systems instead. As one journalist put it, Gillette executives discussed shaving systems 'with the sort of technical gusto one expects from a Boeing engineer.'

2
What can your company be the best in the world at?
This is about taking a realistic look at not just what you do well, but also at what you can do better than anyone else. It is equally important here to understand what you *cannot* be the best in the world at, which requires a healthy dose of honesty. When companies focus on the things that they can do better than any other company, they have the ability to create a massive competitive advantage.

3
What drives your economic engine?
This is not just about simply measuring profit, it is about measuring profit relative to something meaningful. In other words, it means defining your profit denominator (profit per x). This allows you to put money making, which is the end product, into strategic context. Collins points to Wells Fargo, a large regional US bank, which shifted from the category standard of measuring profit per loan to measuring profit per employee as their gold standard. This focus allowed Wells Fargo to be one of the first banks to rely on ATMs and 'stripped down' branches, giving them a huge advantage in a newly deregulated banking market.

For managers, the answers to these three questions will help to focus your strategy and your employees around your company's 'hedgehog concept'. It is much easier to make choices about what strategies to follow, and which ones *not* to follow, if your hedgehog concept is clearly defined.

Re-imagining competition: blue oceans

Having a strong hedgehog concept can only get you so far because it is internally focused. It is about your strengths, your passions and your preferred measurement. Of course, these decisions must also be made within a competitive context, in an effort to create competitive advantage.

W. Chan Kim and Renee Mauborgne, a director and professor respectively at INSEAD, have offered a new framework for viewing competitive business landscapes, which they call 'blue ocean strategy'.[1] Blue oceans are about completely re-imagining the competitive landscape. The goal becomes not just beating your competition, but rather, making them irrelevant.

Most top managers fall into the trap of seeing their business myopically through the lens of engaging their competitors in battle and beating them to gain market share. This is not necessarily a bad thing, but it is extremely limiting when building a business strategy, if it is the only way that you view the competitive landscape. Kim and Mauborgne speculate that undue obsession with current competitors (i.e. focusing on 'winning' in existing markets, or 'red oceans', where the waters are already bloody with each competitor attacking the other) can lead to less success than spending time creating strategies to imagine new, uncluttered markets (i.e. blue oceans, free of back-biting competition).

Value innovation

On one level, most companies have a built-in blue ocean mechanism: research and development in new products. New products often help to create new markets. But blue ocean strategy asks managers to go much further. It asks them to fundamentally re-imagine their core business. One example offered by Kim and Mauborgne is that of Cirque du Soleil. Rather than try to compete with other circuses in an existing, and saturated, market, Cirque du Soleil found a way to create something completely new: a new market with no competitors. They took a core component of the circus – the acrobats – infused it with Las Vegas flair and Broadway-style production, and jettisoned the most expensive cost items – the animals and star performers.

Having left the circus 'red ocean' for the circus-inspired entertainment 'blue ocean', Cirque du Soleil was able to draw huge crowds at ticket prices many times those of a traditional circus, with a lower cost base. This process of lowering costs while adding value to the end user is termed by Kim and Mauborgne as **value innovation**.

Running glossary

value innovation
instead of focusing on competition, making competition irrelevant by creating a leap in value, thereby opening up new and uncontested markets[2]

Cirque du Soleil
Cirque du Soleil used an innovative competitive strategy to reinvent the circus, increasing ticket prices while simultaneously lowering production costs.

So far, we have looked at big-picture approaches to imagining corporate competitive strategy. Underneath the big picture, however, there are strategic plans that need to be developed yearly, quarterly and day-to-day. The average-sized company executes hundreds of strategies every day based on the strategic goals of divisions, brands, departments, groups, geographies and even individual employees. Each of these strategies should be part of a comprehensive and consistent strategic planning process.

The strategic-planning process should always include four key components as set out below.

1

Situation analysis

This is the process of gathering and organizing the information that will be used to set objectives. This step is research-intensive and is often designed around answering specific questions or resolving key issues. Examples of specific key issues are questions such as: 'should we launch the brand in Europe?', or 'can we reposition the brand to appeal to a younger audience?'.

2

Objectives

Once the research has been collected and the key issues answered, it is time to create a clear set of objectives. Objectives answer the question: 'what, specifically, do we need to achieve?'

3

Strategies

Strategies are directly related to objectives. They answer the question: 'how, specifically, are we going to achieve our objectives?'. There may be more than one strategy employed to achieve a specific objective.

4

Measures

This outlines specific data that will be collected to confirm whether or not your strategies are working to achieve your objective(s). Generally, each strategy will have a minimum of one specific success measure.

As a simple example of this process in action, let's speculate about the marketing department of Kraft's savoury spread brand, Vegemite (a big seller in Australia). Assume they have conducted research to see if they could successfully launch the brand in Belgium. Let's speculate that their research showed that three objectives needed to be achieved in order for the brand to be successful. They would need to gain distribution in 50% of Belgian supermarkets, build awareness of the brand from near zero to 60% and communicate a distinct benefit versus existing popular spreads in Belgium (such as Ferrero's Nutella brand).

In order to achieve these objectives, the marketing department would create specific strategies and measures, such as those shown in the table opposite.

Objectives	Strategies	Measures
50% distribution	sell-in trade promotion	The percentage of stores initially stocking the product.
	partnership with local Belgian distributor	The number and quality of shelf placings.
60% unaided awareness	launch advertising campaign	The results of the awareness-tracking study.
	'Vegemite ain't vegetables' consumer promotion	The total number of promotional coupons redeemed.
Distinct benefit	emphasize the health benefits of the B vitamins in Vegemite	Playback of B vitamins by consumers from recall testing (what consumers can remember the day after viewing information about the benefits of B vitamins in Vegemite).
		Consumer survey scores for 'healthy' and 'vitamin-enriched' attributes.

Strategic planning table for speculative example of Kraft's Vegemite spread

Strategy is about making choices.

Michael Porter
University professor at
Harvard Business School

< What is strategy?
The strategic planning process
> The competitive secret weapon: research insights

The power of grids

When developing a strategic plan, one of the simplest and most useful ways to analyse information with a view to making choices clear is to divide the information at hand into a simple 2 × 2 box grid. A grid divides information into clear categories, so that the information can be simply and quickly compared. Here are some examples of common grids used in business today.

SWOT analysis

This grid is extremely helpful in the situation analysis portion of the strategic planning process. It takes the information known about the company, brand or product and breaks it into **S**trengths and **W**eaknesses (which are internal in origin), and **O**pportunities and **T**hreats (which are external). It is often the first place that management starts to see where their competitive advantages and disadvantages lie.

Boston Matrix
The Boston Matrix helps managers treat their product line-up as a portfolio, where different products have different roles to help ensure overall success.

SWOT analysis

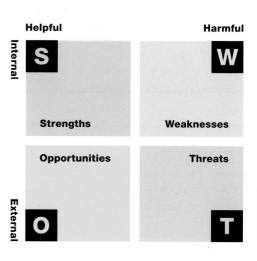

SWOT analysis
The SWOT analysis is a tool that provides an excellent snapshot of a brand's current competitive position. It serves as a strategic baseline.

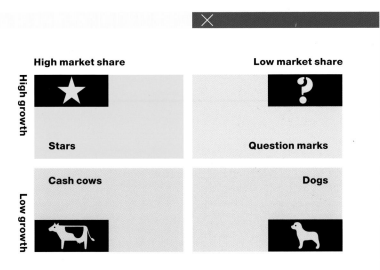

Boston Matrix

The Boston Matrix

This matrix, developed by the Boston Consulting Group, guides strategic planning by helping managers to understand the nature of the product being promoted. Different products have different roles in the company portfolio. They are also in different stages of their product life-cycle. The Boston Matrix helps managers to divide products depending on their market growth and market share.

Brands that are growing rapidly and have high share are considered 'stars' in the portfolio because they bring in a lot of money and growth at the same time.

Brands with low growth but large share are called 'cash cows' because they have dominant positions, and usually need minimal investment to continue making money. Brands with low growth and low share are 'dogs'. Dogs are usually earmarked for termination. Brands with lots of growth but low share are 'question marks'; they may have the potential to become big brands or they might just be fads.

Where a specific brand or product sits in the Boston Matrix will strongly influence the sorts of objectives and strategies that management creates for it.

⟨ What is strategy?
The strategic planning process
⟩ The competitive secret weapon: research insights

Cirque du Soleil's eliminate-reduce-raise-create grid

Eliminate

Star performers

Animal shows

Aisle concession sales

Multiple show arenas

Raise

Unique venue

Reduce

Fun and humour

Thrill and danger

Create

Theme

Refined environment

Multiple productions

Artistic music and dance

Cirque du Soleil's eliminate-reduce-raise-create grid

This grid, created by Kim and Mauborgne, helps managers to identify specific strategic areas that will help to transform the product in the marketplace. It identifies the things that the brand will stop doing (eliminate), do less of (reduce), do more of (raise) and start doing (create). Earlier, we discussed Cirque du Soleil's strategic process in reinventing the circus; above is an example of their grid.[3]

It [the eliminate-reduce-raise-create grid] pushes (companies) to simultaneously pursue differentiation and low costs to break the value-cost trade off.

Kim and Mauborgne
Director and professor
INSEAD

The Pareto principle

Another useful tool in strategic decision making is the Pareto principle, also known as the 80/20 Rule. The principle was named after Italian economist, Vilfredo Pareto, who noticed in the early 1900s that land distribution in Italy was unequal, with 20% of people owning 80% of the land.

The Pareto principle is relevant in all kinds of management and market situations. It is a handy rule of thumb that allows managers to make strategic decisions based on the likelihood that 20% of input will be responsible for 80% of the output. For example, managers can be pretty sure that about 80% of profits will come from 20% of customers. Similarly, they can assume that 20% of staff will create 80% of the headaches, 20% of inventory will take up 80% of the warehouse space, 20% of the work will consume 80% of the manpower and so on.

The Pareto principle is a reminder for managers to focus on the 20% that matters. If 20% of input produces 80% of your results, it helps to identify those things and to really focus on them. When your resources are focused on the 20% that matters, it is easy to avoid the waste and inefficiency arising from the 80% that provides little more than distraction.

〈 The strategic planning process
The competitive secret weapon: research insights
〉 Case study: Apple's iPod and iPhone

Good processes, such as using the strategic planning process, SWOT analyses and the 80/20 rule, can help focus competitive strategy development. But nothing can replace the importance of having insights into your customers (and potential customers) that your competitors lack. Unique customer insights can lead to new products, product positionings and creative advertising ideas that stand out from the competitive pack. Products that stand out and 'speak' to consumers' needs usually command higher prices, or higher market share at the same price point.

In order to garner insights into consumer needs, marketers use both *quantitative and qualitative research* techniques.

Quantitative research

In marketing terms, quantitative research is about gathering data on such things as consumer needs, attitudes and purchase patterns. The key is to get a large enough number of people, called a **sample**, to be able to project the answers across larger populations. For example, when done properly, a survey of a few thousand teenagers in a number of key markets can give you a good picture of the attitudes of teens on a regional or even national basis.

The refined practice of 'sampling' made it immensely easier for marketers and media owners to gain insights into their entire market. Sampling was perfected by George Gallup in the 1930s. The technique came out of his PhD thesis and was built on the statistical theories of Jacob Bernoulli, the seventeenth century Swiss mathematician. As Gallup explained it:

'Suppose there are seven thousand white beans and three thousand black beans well churned in a barrel. If you scoop out one hundred of them, you'll get approximately seventy white beans and thirty black in your hand, and the range of possible error can be computed mathematically. As long as the barrel contains many more beans than your handful, the proportion will remain within that margin of error 997 times out of 1000.' **4**

Running glossary

sample
a portion of the population representative of the whole

When done regularly over time, quantitative research is an excellent way to measure trends. It helps to answer the question: 'what is my target audience thinking and/or doing?'.

The most common form of quantitative research is a *survey*. A survey can be done by mail, over the phone, online or in person. Because each respondent is answering the same questions, often on a five- or seven-point scale, it becomes easy to calculate and compare the responses across geographies, demographic groups and so on. Relationships between answers to specific questions and how they relate to answers to other specific questions can also be compared.

Quantitative research is vital in marketing, yet it often gives little competitive advantage. This is because competitive companies often use the same syndicated research results and/or conduct similar surveys about similar products showing the same trends. So, not having great quantitative research would be a competitive disadvantage, but having it does not always put you far ahead. There are exceptions, though and some smart marketers, such as Procter & Gamble and Unilever, have made surveys a fine art.

Procter & Gamble: creative research

One company that consistently uses quantitative research in interesting and creative ways is Procter & Gamble (P&G). P&G recently conducted a massive survey to understand women's emotional feelings about 'bad hair days'. Building on a previous study where they found that 'bad hair negatively influences self esteem, brings out social insecurities and causes people to concentrate on the negative aspects of themselves', they found that women also felt less 'hostile', 'ashamed', 'nervous', guilty' or 'jittery' depending on which hair-care products they used.[5] These were deep insights that helped P&G find unique product positionings in hair care.

< The strategic planning process
The competitive secret weapon: research insights
> Case study: Apple's iPod and iPhone

Qualitative research

Qualitative research is not about numbers (i.e. sample size) or projecting answers across large populations. It is about understanding the deeper psychological processes that drive the product's purchase. It is about consumers' attitudes towards your brand and competitive brands. It helps answer the question: 'why is my target audience feeling and acting that way?'.

Qualitative research is personal. It delves into emotions. In this realm, marketers can often tease out insights into consumer behaviour that their competitors do not possess. Great qualitative research is built around intimate discussions. The goal is to listen to consumers rather than to give them preset responses from which to choose. This is often done in one-on-one interviews (one interviewer and one respondent) or in focus groups (one interviewer with a small group of people).

Jon Steel, who spent many years as vice-chairman and director of account planning at the advertising agency Goodby, Siverstein & Partners, believes that qualitative research is best when it adheres to the rules of 'simplicity, common sense and creativity'. Creativity in research often means finding the best way for consumers to get in touch with their deepest feelings.

Steel recounts the story of Porsche. Rather than ask Porsche owners to describe how they felt about their cars, researchers asked them to draw their feelings instead.

At first, this usually scared respondents, who claimed they could not draw well. But once they started, it began to bring out the child in them.

Their drawings explained their deep emotions better than words ever could. In the case of Porsche, owners rarely drew the car. What they drew instead were winding mountain roads or the road from the driver's point of view. What they were communicating was that Porsche is not just about sleek good looks and raw horsepower: it is about a performance driving experience. They were communicating, deep down, that they really loved the pure joy of driving.

Emotion

Gaining insights is critically important because, as neurologist Donald Caine points out: 'The essential difference between emotion and reason is that emotion leads to action while reason leads to conclusions.' Tapping into the emotions of your customers can lead to a lot of action, and a lot of sales, at your competitor's expense.

When conducting qualitative research, as well as listening to what the participants openly say, Jon Steel believes it is just as important to listen to what they are *not* saying and to observe their body language carefully. When there are lines of discussion that participants avoid, it is telling you something. That something may be wonderful or horrible for your product, but you need to know what it is.

Likewise, people's body language often belies what they are saying. They may be saying what you want to hear, but if they have their arms and legs tightly crossed and a stern face, you may have a problem.

Steel uses the example of a focus group where respondents are shown a TV commercial. While watching the commercial they lean forward with bright eyes and laugh heartily, yet when asked what they think, they stop smiling and say something like: 'I think some people may be offended by that.' He notes: 'Their own body language clearly stated that *they* were not offended by it. They were involved, they got it, and they liked it, yet their comments immediately afterward would suggest the opposite.'

Research is a mix of science, art and intuition. Once the data has been collected, and the specific answers logged, we need to appreciate that people often tell us more through their gaze, attention and posture than through their words. Smart marketers use a combination of quantitative and qualitative techniques to discover what their customers and potential customers are thinking, feeling and doing.

Xploring: ethnography

One increasingly popular type of qualitative research is ethnography, which often entails getting involved in participants' lives to such a degree that you can observe them in their natural habitats (e.g. their homes), as opposed to a research facility.

Sandy Thompson, author of *One in a Billion*, used a unique form of ethnography called 'Xploring' when trying to gain insights into the newly emerging consumer market in China in the 1990s. She and her team put on hiking boots and backpacks and journeyed across China, developing a series of intimate portraits of some of the individuals who make up the world's most populous nation. They created a snapshot of what it means to be Chinese in the new millennium, interacting with people on a personal level without any questionnaire at all.

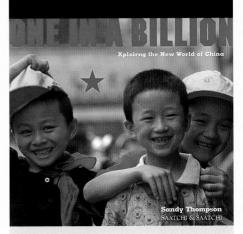

One in a Billion

Case study: Apple's iPod and iPhone

Apple is a popular case study in business and marketing books. They are perhaps the world's most consistently innovative company. Over the years their products, such as the Macintosh, the iMac and even the once reviled Newton, have consistently broken new ground.

Through the lens of competitive strategy, no moves by Apple have been more impactful than the introduction of both the iPod and the iPhone. What made these products so competitively overwhelming were some important strategic decisions, which outflanked the competition and created 'blue oceans' for Apple.

The strategic decision that led to the extreme success of the iPod had little to do with the product itself. MP3 players were increasingly available from a number of quality manufacturers, and the iPod was not even considered the best one available, having a weak reputation for battery performance.

What made iPod a huge competitive success was the development of its symbiotic sister product iTunes. iTunes had a huge library of songs, standardized pricing and an easy-to-use interface that made downloading songs a breeze versus other MP3 players' myriad music websites. It caught on so quickly that 'iPod' soon became a generic name for any MP3 player.

Great market research and insights

Apple's advantage underlines the importance of great market research and insights. Average consumers were looking for a much simpler approach to downloading songs, not just a music-recording device as a single offering. Apple discovered that people wanted a *system* that combined the recording device and the music download website. People did not want to surf numerous sites looking for songs or worry that some sites would not work with their recorders. That was a powerful consumer insight, the result no doubt of the combination of great qualitative and quantitative research.

The iPhone has sold over 50 million units worldwide, and the launch of the iPhone 4 promises to continue the product's rapid sales growth (selling 600,000 units in its first day!). Like the iPod, the iPhone's success was the result of great strategic decisions made by Apple management early in its development.

The iPhone was built around a user interface driven by applications, or 'apps'. Apps are specialized downloadable computer programs that work like built-in websites to accomplish specific tasks, such as providing weather reports, tracking flight information or providing a game to play.

Apps were not new to the computing world, but they were a relatively fresh approach in the world of mobile phones. Using apps was a key strategic decision, but what made iPhone's blue ocean a reality was the decision to 'open source' the development of applications.

When developing products, Apple has historically been religious about creating and controlling the driving software. But they soon realized that the iPhone could only deliver its promise to consumers if a vast array of apps were available to download. Millions of different users with hundreds of different personal interests meant that Apple needed a comprehensive library of applications, not just ten or twenty.

In order to develop this library quickly, so as not to delay the launch of the product or lose the competitive market window, Apple agreed that any software company, big or small, that met its strict specifications, would be allowed to develop applications for the iPhone. With dozens of Silicon Valley companies working around the clock to provide software, Apple was able to meet the market need with an avalanche of applications, which left other mobile phone manufacturers gasping for air at the thought of competing with the iPhone. To date, iPhone users have downloaded over five billion apps; the average iPhone user has about fifty on their phone.

The success of the iPhone/apps combination has led to another big competitive move by Apple: the launch of the iPad tablet computer. The iPad, which uses a similar apps-driven interface, sold one million units twice as fast as the first iPod, and sold three million units in 80 days, restrained only by Apple's ability to produce more of them.

The iPod completely changed the way people approach music.

Karl Lagerfeld
Fashion designer

< The competitive secret weapon: research insights
Case study: Apple's iPod and iPhone
> Questions and exercises

Leadership

Apple can also teach us a lot about leadership. Steve Jobs, Apple's CEO, has been the company's catalyst. His personal vision, outstanding ability to simplify complex ideas into simple thoughts and his tireless work ethic have helped to keep Apple's employees focused on innovation. From the introduction of the Macintosh in 1984 – the first home computer with a graphical user interface allowing users to interact with items on the screen – to the 2010 launch of the applications-driven iPad, Apple continues to deliver on its mission, and Jobs' vision.

How important has his personal leadership been? The company was successful and growing when he left the CEO role to start a new venture in 1985. Afterwards, its fortunes sagged, prompting his return as CEO in 1996. Since then, Apple's revenue has more than doubled, an amazing feat for a company that was already very large.

Question 1

Are there any other products or categories that you think could benefit by offering consumers a product 'system' rather than just a single product?

Question 2

How long do you think Apple's blue oceans can last before the water starts to become bloody with competition?

Question 3

What can we learn from the fact that the iPhone was inspired by computer software, which then in turn inspired the iPad computer?

Here's to the crazy ones, the misfits, the rebels, the troublemakers, the round pegs in the square holes... the ones who see things differently.

Apple commercial

Apple's iPad
The iPad is the latest in a series of superb strategic moves by Apple. The combination of innovative product form – a tablet computer – and embracing apps on the computing platform as well as on the mobile platform bode well for Apple's continued competitive health.

Questions and exercises

>

Discussion questions

1
Why is it important to look at both internal and external factors when developing a SWOT analysis?

2
In the Boston Matrix, what is the best outcome for 'question marks'? What is the worst?

3
Are there certain research questions for which it is not important to do qualitative research in addition to quantitative research?

Exercises

1
Create a SWOT analysis for Mercedes-Benz. Does it make you think differently about the company, its products and its future opportunities?

2
Break into teams. Imagine that you are introducing a new fashion clothing line. Map out specific types of quantitative and qualitative research techniques that you plan to employ to gain unique consumer insights. Compare the similarities and differences of the different approaches.

3
Assume that your number one objective for launching a new product is to get people to try it for the first time. List specific strategies that you might try. What specific measures will you look at to see if the strategies are working effectively?

Summary

Competition is about strategy. Superior strategies create competitive separation and help products to win in the marketplace. There are a number of specific tools, such as the SWOT analysis, that allow managers and their teams to quickly and effectively sift through information and to distil it into effective strategies. Great strategies also include consumer insights to make sure that they will resonate with the people who will buy the product.

Suggested further reading

Collins, J. (2001) *Good to Great: Why Some Companies Make the Leap... and others don't.* (New York: HarperCollins Publishers Inc.)

Kim, W. C. and R. Mauborgne. (2005) *Blue Ocean Strategy: How to Create Uncontested Market Space and Make the Competition Irrelevant.* (Boston: Harvard Business School Publishing)

Steel, J. (1998) *Truth, Lies, and Advertising: The Art of Account Planning.* (New York: John Wiley & Sons)

Thompson, S. (2006) *One in a Billion: Xploring the New World of China.* (New York: powerHouse Books)

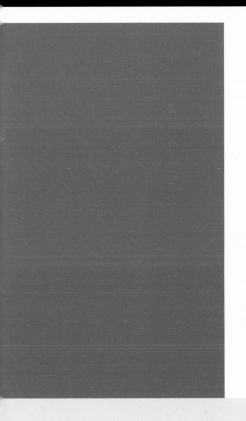

This chapter focuses on the economic value of brands. It discusses the ability of great brands to command higher prices in the marketplace, provide added value to customers, and deliver higher returns for company shareholders. We will look at the importance of 'positioning' as the foundation of a differentiated brand.

There are many theories of branding and many strategies to make a brand stand out in the marketplace. We will explore a number of popular and controversial branding theories, including 'lighthouse brands', 'challenger brands' and 'Lovemarks'. The chapter ends with a case study of a powerful brand that has differentiated itself in the market and which has consistently commanded higher prices than its competition: Tiffany & Co.

Brands are much more than just products. Branding is the process of lending special meaning to a product in a way that results in consumers clearly differentiating the product from similar products, and perceiving it to provide *added value*. Differentiation and the perception of added value equate to competitive advantage in the marketplace by creating brand preference with consumers.

Brands can add value in many different ways. They can have a better price, wider distribution, higher performance or better design, for example. Superiority in any of these areas can make the brand more attractive, and worth more money, to consumers. Such areas of differentiation support rational thought processes when choosing products.

Brands can also add value based on their image. This type of differentiation taps into the consumer's emotional thought processes. A brand can differentiate itself, for example, by looking 'cooler' than other brands. This is a strategy used by most fashion brands. Fashion brands that appear cool and stylish succeed over those that do not.

Brand image

A strong brand image can also be created through a single-minded focus on one unique aspect of a brand. Repetition of this idea over time creates a strong image with consumers that the brand has added value in that area. Most great brands combine product superiority with a strong image, giving consumers both rational and emotional reasons to prefer that brand. Apple does this extremely well by consistently introducing breakthrough products, while also playing to consumers' emotions in their advertising.

Creating added brand value and strong brand image are primary responsibilities for marketing managers because they create brand preference with consumers. The stronger the brand preference, the less likely consumers will be to substitute it with another brand. And, as we learned in Chapter 1 (see page 22), this ability to make demand for your product inelastic means that you can make more money from your product(s) than your competitors can.

Running glossary

brand equity
the total financial value of the brand

shareholder equity
a firm's total assets minus its total liabilities

When brands are built consistently over a long period of time, such as Coca-Cola or Walt Disney, the total financial value of the brand (often called **brand equity**) can be enormous, even outweighing the value of all of the company's actual physical assets. Interbrand, which publishes a yearly list of the most valuable brands, lists the most valuable global brands as follows:[1]

Brand (2010)	**Value** ($ millions)
Coca-Cola	70,452
IBM	64,727
Microsoft	60,895
Google	43,557
General Electric	42,808

Great managers build great brands. They know that a great product with a great brand image can generate many times more revenue than a great product that does not capture the hearts and minds of the consumer. They also know that brand equity delivers something important: **shareholder equity**. Improved shareholder equity means that the people who own stock in your company get a greater return on their investment. Shareholders are ultimately the ones who decide if management is doing a good job (with their money).

Volvo: an image of safety

Volvo automobiles are a good example of a brand that consistently focuses on a single positive attribute: safety. Although there is no conclusive evidence that Volvo's cars are consistently safer than any number of other quality car brands, their steadfast focus on their safety image has left an indelible impression on consumers. For example, in 2010 Consumer Reports conducted a survey asking car owners which brand they considered best for safety. The results were:

Brand	Per cent
Volvo	73
Ford	22
Subaru	21
Toyota	18
Honda	17

Great brands usually start with a positioning statement. Made popular by the work of Al Reis and Jack Trout in the 1970s, and memorialized in their 1981 book *Positioning: The Battle for your Mind*, positioning statements are now de rigueur for marketers trying to build distinctive brands. The concept behind positioning statements is that consumers are continuously inundated with thousands of advertising and marketing messages (according to some estimates, people see over 3,000 advertising messages per day).

A good summary of Reis and Trout's idea is:

'Consumers cope with information overload by oversimplifying, and are likely to shut out anything inconsistent with their knowledge and experience. In an over-communicated environment, the advertiser should present a simplified message and make that message consistent with what the consumer already believes by focusing on the perceptions of the consumer rather than on the reality of the product.' **2**

Simplicity of communication

Positioning is an attempt to create simplicity of communication. A good positioning statement boils down the product's unique benefit or 'point of view' (sometimes called its 'value proposition') into its most basic form. This simplicity helps consumers to remember the product and, just as importantly, allows the people working on the product to keep focused on simple, consistent messages. Over time, these messages can transform products into brands.

The exact structure of a positioning statement varies by company. A common approach is as follows:

For **target audience** our brand is the **frame of reference** that **has a unique benefit or point of view**.

If the unique benefit or point of view is not self-evident, it will often be followed by a 'reason to believe' (i.e. 'because…').

A good example of this approach can be seen in the quick-serve chicken restaurant Chick-fil-A. Their positioning statement is:

For **people in a hurry** Chick-fil-A is the **fast food restaurant** that **consistently serves America's best-loved chicken**. **3**

In the fast-food category, Chick-fil-A's singular focus on chicken versus hamburgers helps to make them unique.

…if you've actually tried to achieve a position in the marketplace, you know that the gulf between theory and practice can be distressingly wide.

George P. Dovel
CEO
Dovel Group

Chick-fil-A
Chick-fil-A used a simple positioning statement to help them develop this award-winning campaign, which helps them to stand out as a distinctive brand in their category. The campaign has been successful on an emotional level, too. People love the cows, which serve as the campaign's foil. In fact, people love the cows so much that Chick-fil-A has devoted a whole section of their website to them.

George Dovel, an ex-Hewlett-Packard executive who founded Dovel Group, a marketing consultancy to hi-tech companies, has developed a detailed eight-step process for creating positioning statements. His process includes steps such as: 'identify the attributes customers use to differentiate products'; 'understand the positionings of competitive products'; and 'test it to make sure you can effectively communicate the positioning statement'.[4]

For a tool whose sole purpose is to create simplicity, a rigorous eight-step process might seem like overkill. But Dovel explains: 'It might seem like a lot of work to develop one little sentence. But everything you do – from developing the product to writing the ad copy – will be much easier if you've nailed the positioning statement up front.'[5]

Stickiness

Simplicity and consistency of message leads to 'sticky' branding. Stickiness is about the ability of a message to stay with a consumer over time (i.e. the message is easy to recall). Sticky messages lead to a greater degree of product trial. If the product delivers on the promise, then the sticky message reinforces that the decision to buy the product was a good one and leads to repeat purchases.

Lovemarks

We learned in the previous chapter that insights into the emotions of consumers can be the most powerful of all. Kevin Roberts, worldwide CEO of advertising agency Saatchi & Saatchi, used this as the cornerstone of a new theory of branding. He called his theory 'lovemarks'.

To Roberts' way of thinking, products initially evolved into trademarks. As they became more trusted and respected over time, trademarks then developed into brands. He believes that we have now reached a stage beyond brands, where the highest products in the pecking order do more than evoke feelings of trust or respect: they even arouse feelings of love. Roberts recommends that today's brands start measuring themselves using a new tool: the love-respect axis (see diagram opposite).

Respected products deliver what great brands have always delivered: performance, trust and reputation. Lovemarks deliver these things plus mystery, sensuality and intimacy. Lovemarks create an emotional bond that goes beyond respect.[6]

Lovemarks are the products left standing when you ask consumers the question: 'Can you imagine life without this brand?'. For many consumers, products such as the Volkswagen Beetle, Coca-Cola, Diesel Jeans, Apple Macintosh and Clinique pass the test. They are products people not only respect, but about which people tell stories to their friends. They are brands that consumers use to navigate their emotional landscape.

Can we put a specific value on 'love'? Between 1996 and 2006, research on companies that people said they loved returned 1,184% to their investors compared to 122% for the S&P 500 average.[7]

Emotions are important determinants of economic behaviour, more than rationality.

Dr Daniel Kahneman
Nobel Laureate in Economics
2002

The love-respect axis

Brands
Low love
High respect

Lovemarks
High love
High respect

Love

Respect

Products
Low love
Low respect

Fads
High love
Low respect

The love-respect axis
The love-respect axis allows managers to plot their products versus other competitors in their category to see which brands consumers connect with emotionally as well as rationally. Lovemarks are brands that garner both high respect and love.

Private label brands

A significant challenge to top brands has been the consolidation of distribution into bigger and bigger retailers (sometimes called 'big box stores'). These retailers not only have strong negotiating power on price, they have also learned how to use their relationships with their customers to build their own powerful brands.

For example, two of the biggest retailers in the US, Costco and Macy's, have created some high-profile private label brands that are lovemarks for many consumers because they combine top brand quality with significantly lower prices. Costco has created a whole line of products under the 'Kirkland' label that offers everything from shampoo to dress shirts. Macy's has created a stable of quasi-fashion products, including men's suits under the Alfani brand, 'American Rag', which offers denims and casual clothes for young people, and 'Charter Club', offering women's casual clothes.

< Lovemarks
Lighthouse brands and thought leadership
> Case study: Tiffany & Co. – a powerful brand

Adam Morgan knows a lot about branding. As planning director for advertising agency giant TBWA in Europe, the US and Latin America, working on brands such as Nissan, Apple, Energizer and Absolut, he developed a theory about 'challenger brands'. At its core, the theory states: 'To be number one, you need to think and act like number two.' He points out that number one brands, which he calls 'big fish', are fundamentally different from smaller brands (i.e. 'little fish').

Big fish have the advantage of critical mass. They often have dramatically higher awareness, share of shopping, sales, loyalty and profitability. In short, it is very good to be a big fish. However, big fish often become intensely conservative in their decision making. They are trying to protect their advantage. They don't want to make too many risky moves that might impact negatively upon their market dominance. Interestingly, their reluctance to take risks is often the exact opposite of the type of decision making that got them to the number one position in the first place.

Smaller brands, on the other hand, need to take more risks. They need to maintain a challenger attitude in order to stand out and gain a share from the big fish. Challenger brands are often far more dynamic in their thinking. Because of this, Morgan believes that number one brands will only maintain their dominance if they remember to behave in the same way as they did when they were number two.

Two goals that Morgan sets out for challenger brands are:

1

to build a lighthouse identity,

2

assume 'thought leadership' for the category.

Lighthouse brands

Creating a 'lighthouse' brand is about avoiding the 'me-too' approach of identifying a consumer problem and positioning yourself as the one who solves that problem. This is the approach of many brand leaders, so it provides little competitive advantage. It may even provide a competitive disadvantage, since the brand leader has more awareness in this area.

Lighthouse brands do not navigate by the consumer. Rather, they focus on themselves, inviting consumers to navigate by them. Just like a real lighthouse, the brand then has a chance to be seen clearly in the fog and to stand out in the marketplace.

According to Morgan, lighthouse brands have four main characteristics, as outlined below.

1
Self-referential identity
They are focused on telling us where *they* stand and what *they* are all about.

2
Emotion
They focus on making an emotional, as well as a rational, connection with consumers.

3
Intensity
They are vivid and intense about everything that they do and say.

4
Salience
They are intrusive. People cannot help but notice them. Sometimes they are even audacious.[8]

Thought leadership

Lighthouse brands try to create 'thought leadership' in their categories, which justifies their salience and self-reference. Without thought leadership, self-referential brands can be seen as shallow and meaningless.

Thought leaders break the conventions of the category, creating a new dialogue with consumers. They often break conventions of representation too. For example, Virgin Airlines, through their name alone, created a new thought relationship with flyers. They often break conventions of medium. Wonderbra broke with convention to feature their sexy push-up bras on outdoor boards, rather than within the pages of women's fashion magazines.

Lighthouse brands also break conventions of product experience. In the 1990s, UK food retailer Tesco took on the number one brand, Sainsbury's, by changing the food shopping experience — as opposed to just having a great selection of food. They paid particular attention to mothers shopping with small children. They introduced such benefits as priority parking for people with small children, baby-changing facilities and staff to pack your bags. In 1995, Tesco overtook Sainsbury's as Britain's biggest food retailer and have dominated the market ever since.

‹ Lighthouse brands and thought leadership
Case study: Tiffany & Co. – a powerful brand
› Questions and exercises

This chapter has focused on tools that managers use to build great brands and how those brands, in turn, build great returns for shareholders in the company. There are many brands that have delivered this kind of value, including Guinness, Cadbury, Nescafé and Coca-Cola.

Few brands, however, have delivered such simple and consistent branding for as long a time period, or created such a degree of shareholder value, as Tiffany & Co. The company was founded in 1837 and was a great brand 100 years before many of today's great brands were even born. Tiffany's represents a monumental achievement in terms of building a powerful brand and, more importantly, of then keeping it relevant and sought after decade after decade.

How many brands are as prestigious today as they were 50 years ago? Looking back to 1958, Tiffany was such a powerful symbol of luxury that it was the centrepiece of a best-selling novel by Truman Capote, which was made into one of Hollywood's most unforgettable movies: *Breakfast at Tiffany's*. Would 'Breakfast at Bulgari' have had such cultural resonance, then or now?

Tiffany blue

One of Tiffany's most important marketing decisions was made by its founder, Charles Lewis Tiffany, when he chose a powder blue colour to represent the brand. The colour, now known as 'Tiffany blue', adorns the paper and boxes that wrap and enclose Tiffany products, as well as the brand's advertising. The Tiffany-blue box, paired with a white satin ribbon and bow, has now become one of the world's most recognized symbols of luxury. James Mansour, head of Mansour design, a New York retail brand consultancy, notes:

'[The blue box] represents refinement, luxury, elegance, good taste and quality, and it confers status on both the person who gives it and the person who receives it.' **9**

Picking a colour may not seem like such a weighty management decision. But what Tiffany knew decades before it became known as 'branding' was that products can take ownership over symbols, ideas or objects and endow them with unique associations and special meanings.

Similarly, Michelin has given meaning to a man made of white tyres; Energizer has given meaning to a battery-powered toy rabbit; and Marlboro has borrowed the cowboy and made it an icon of smoking, of all things.

Breakfast at Tiffany's
Tiffany & Co's incomparable branding has put it at the centre of our image of luxury, whether 50 years ago, as the inspiration for *Breakfast at Tiffany's*, or today.

< Lighthouse brands and thought leadership
Case study: Tiffany & Co. – a powerful brand
> Questions and exercises

Ownership

'Ownership' is an important word. When a brand can own an image, a sound, an emotion, an icon or even a colour, it becomes shorthand for the brand's unique 'promise'. No other brand can be associated with the same promise in quite the same way. Once ingrained, the brand device also becomes a **mnemonic** memory trigger. When consumers see it, feel it or hear it they get the message and remember the brand to the detriment of its competitors.

When people see a blue Tiffany box, they value what is inside more highly, and they are willing to spend more money for it (sometimes a lot more) than for the exact same item in a different box. The perceived value is higher when it comes in a Tiffany box versus even a Cartier box. The effect of the blue box is highly emotional, which is why Tiffany & Co. fits right in with the definition of a lovemark.

Because so much of Tiffany's brand equity is related to the blue box, they take its quality and handling very seriously. For example, every employee must attend a class to learn the exact art of tying the ribbon so that the box lays flat.[10] And the training doesn't end there. The blue box encompasses in a simple image the entire Tiffany experience. To make sure that this experience is up to standard, new employees undergo six to eight weeks of intense product knowledge and skills training. They must even pass a written test before ever greeting a customer.[11]

Continued success

The Tiffany brand has prospered for generations, in large part due to their understanding of the subtle branding power of a simple box, its distinctive blue colour and a white satin ribbon. And their branding power has never been more evident. In 2009, in the midst of a worldwide economic crisis, Tiffany's sales fell 5%. Yet as markets started to recover, Tiffany & Co. reported a whopping 22% increase in the first quarter of 2010. At the same time, they reiterated their plan to open 16 new stores (to add to their 223 existing stores in 22 countries) and to launch a new leather goods collection.[12]

Running glossary

mnemonic
relating to, assisting, or intended to assist the memory

Tiffany's blue box
Tiffany & Co. have taken brand
ownership of a colour – Tiffany blue.
This colour has come to uniquely
represent the brand, its promise,
and its experience.

Question 1
Can you think of any other brands
that have created ownership over
something as simple as a colour or
a sound?

Question 2
Cartier is a key competitor of
Tiffany & Co. It has its own distinctive
red box. It also has a history dating
back to the 1800s. So, why have
Cartier not been able to brand red
with the same perceived value as
Tiffany blue?

Question 3
Do you think that Tiffany & Co's
training programme is a bit over
the top? Does it really matter how the
ribbons are tied?

$\langle$ Case study: Tiffany & Co. – a powerful brand
Questions and exercises
$\rangle$

Discussion questions

1

What is the 'stickiest' advertising message that you have seen lately?

2

Can you think of a brand that has recently broken conventions of representation, medium or product experience?

3

Which companies would you like to be a shareholder in based on the strength of their brands?

Exercises

1

Choose an existing brand that is not number one in its category. List three ways it could add value versus the category leader.

2

Choose another brand. Based on what you know about it, try to write the brand's positioning statement.

3

Think about the automotive category. Place the brands that you know on the 'love-respect' axis. Which ones are lovemarks, which are fads and so on?

Summary

Successful marketing infuses products with values, ideas and images that make them hard to substitute with other products because consumers become emotionally engaged with them. This is the process of turning a product into a brand. Once established, a brand can command significantly higher prices and generate economic value way beyond their actual production value. Successful managers know that brands matter, a lot.

Suggested further reading

Morgan, A. (1999) *Eating the Big Fish: How Challenger Brands Can Compete Against Brand Leaders*. (New York: John Wiley & Sons, Inc.)

Dovel, G. P. (July, 1990) Stake It Out: Positioning Success, Step by Step. *Business Marketing*, pp. 43–51

Ries, A. and J. Trout. (2001) *Positioning: The Battle for Your Mind*. (New York: McGraw Hill)

Sisodia, R., Sheth, J. and D. Wolfe. (2007) *Firms of Endearment: How World-Class Companies Profit from Passion and Purpose*. (New Jersey: Wharton School Publishing)

This chapter provides insights into one of the most difficult aspects of management: managing people. Great management is equal parts culture creation, communication, conflict resolution and politics. Dealing with employees and their issues can be either the most rewarding or the most depressing part of being a manager.

We will review some basic psychological principles that help managers to understand why people do the things that they do. We will also look at a variety of tools and philosophies that can help managers to navigate the sometimes stormy seas of employee relations. Ultimately, this chapter hopes to enable managers to inspire their employees to achieve great things, together.

Psychology is the science that studies mental processes and behaviour. For managers, an understanding of basic psychology can help them to interpret and understand the actions of employees. It can also help them to devise the best strategies for motivating them. There are countless psychological theories, but two of the most important, and useful, come from two of the most famous names in the history of psychology: B. F. Skinner, who developed theories of behaviourism; and Sigmund Freud, who developed theories of the unconscious mind and the ego.

Skinner's theories of behaviourism focus on understanding people's actions as a function of specific environmental factors that reinforce specific behaviours. Productive behaviour can be repeatedly stimulated by providing positive reinforcement (e.g. giving someone an award for a great sales month), or by removing a negative event (e.g. avoiding criticizing an employee who has made a mistake, so that they won't be too nervous to take a risk next time). Punishment (e.g. giving an employee a pay cut for bad performance) is also a form of reinforcement.

Understanding that there are different strategies for promoting productive employee behaviour is important. Many managers use one approach (e.g. punishment) because it either fits their personality or is consistent with how they were raised. Deciding which strategy is best-suited to a specific situation – and employee – is an important management function.

Skinner believed that the ability of specific events to reinforce specific behaviours over time (i.e. 'environmental histories of reinforcing consequences') was more important than introspection or cognition.

Freud was on a very different track from Skinner. Whereas Skinner was interested in what people did versus how they felt, Freud was focused on feelings and emotions. He was interested in feelings that we are aware of, but he was especially interested in those feelings that we are not aware of: the ones below the threshold of consciousness.

Freud mapped out the human psyche into three facets: the id, the ego and the super-ego. The id is the part of the psyche that desires personal pleasure. It tells you to get what you want regardless of consequences. The super-ego is highly moral, telling you to do the right thing regardless of what it means for your well-being. The ego is the rational part of the psyche that wrestles between the equal impracticality of the id and the super-ego.

Why are the id, the ego and the super-ego important? Different people rationalize between them in different ways. Some people are more focused on their own needs; others are more focused on the needs of others. Managers need to recognize that each individual has different priorities, emotions and motivations.

Considering Skinner and Freud together, successful managers create strategies for motivating their workforce as a whole, decide what approach they will take to reinforce that behaviour over time and how they will motivate each individual – given their unique ego – to do their best for the team.

The executives who ignited the transformations from good to great did not first figure out where to drive the bus and then get people to take it there. No, they first got the right people on the bus.

Jim Collins
Good to Great

Job number one: hire good people

Jim Collins, author of *Good to Great*, did an exhaustive study of companies that had transformed themselves from good companies with good performance, to great companies with great performance. He found that the cornerstone of such transformation was having a group of dedicated and disciplined employees. As he put it, companies that want to be great ask: 'First who… then what.' He also noted that great companies put more emphasis on character attributes than on skills, education, experience or knowledge.

In my previous company, Saatchi & Saatchi, we were relentless about identifying the right people. One method that we used was deceptively simple. We identified three basic attributes that were characteristic of the kind of people who thrive in our culture. They were: 'passionate, competitive and restless.' We called them 'ideas people'.

Our company was focused on creativity, and without passion it is impossible to foster creativity. We were in a highly competitive industry, where winning 25% of your new business pitches would be considered a pretty good track record. We needed people who wanted to win! Finally, we wanted people who were always looking to move ahead, who wanted to learn new things. Our industry was in the midst of tremendous change due to digital media. We wanted restless people who would never be satisfied with their current knowledge or job.

Our company also conducted an in-depth psychological analysis of people who fit the profile. From it, we created a specific list of telltale signs to look for when interviewing for 'ideas people'; including 'intuition', 'optimism', 'free-mind abilities', 'openness to stimuli' and 'nonconformity'. We even created specific interview questions to discern whether candidates met these criteria. For example, a simple question that sheds a lot of light on someone's openness to stimuli is to ask them which famous people they would like to meet and why. A simple question to discern their optimism is to ask them what they learned from a failed advertising campaign that they worked on.

These three simple words – competitive, passionate, restless – and the materials created to identify people who displayed these characteristics, helped more managers to hire more great people to our company than ever before.

Running glossary

value system
set of values adopted or developed by a person or organization as a standard to guide its behaviour in all situations

Culture as management

It is not possible for any manager, or group of managers, to motivate every employee all of the time, or to deal with all of their myriad daily challenges and issues. Therefore, once you have hired the right people, it is important to create a culture of success.

Creating a culture of success hinges on communicating the values of the company and inculcating them into the **value system** of all the people who work for the company. When a corporate culture is strong enough, employees motivate each other and solve many of their own problems because the guidelines are clear; and the guidelines are supported by all of the people around them. This allows management to focus on creating a vision, setting objectives and formulating big picture strategies.

One example of a terrific culture is the aircraft and defence company Lockheed Martin. According to their website, they insist that each employee 'do what's right', 'respect others' and 'perform with excellence'.

Do what's right

'We are committed to the highest standards of ethical conduct in all that we do. We believe that honesty and integrity engender trust, which is the cornerstone of our business. We abide by the laws of the United States and other countries in which we do business, we strive to be good citizens and we take responsibility for our actions.

Respect others

'We recognize that our success as an enterprise depends on the talent, skills and expertise of our people and our ability to function as a tightly integrated team. We appreciate our diversity and believe that respect – for our colleagues, customers, partners, and all those with whom we interact – is an essential element of all positive and productive business relationships.

Perform with excellence

'We understand the importance of our missions and the trust our customers place in us. With this in mind, we strive to excel in every aspect of our business and approach every challenge with a determination to succeed.' [1]

When employees absorb simple values, a strong culture is created which focuses on the right things without a lot of management oversight. When certain employees *do not*, it is critical for management to identify them and to either reform them or let them go. Everybody on the bus needs to be driving in the same direction.

Managing across cultures

In 1988, I moved from New York to Japan to begin an 11-year posting overseas. During those years, I managed local employees, first in Japan, then in Hong Kong and finally in Australia.

I had expected that there would be a lot of cultural learning to do in places like Japan and Hong Kong: the linguistic and ethnic differences were wide and obvious. What surprised me was that there were just as many management challenges in Australia as in Asia. The fact that we spoke the same language and shared a similar ethnic background did not make us as alike as I had expected. I had three wonderful and successful years in Australia (due in part to the cultural sensitivities that I had learned working in Asia), but the fact remains that many American managers struggle there.

I could write a book about the differences in outlook between Americans and Australians: American fierce individualism and stratified class structure versus Australian egalitarianism and communal 'mate-ship', for example. The bigger point, however, is that in our increasingly global society, managers from many countries are now managing people in different countries from their own. A manager from California may manage a call centre in Costa Rica; a manager in India may manage a web-development team in Great Britain; or a manager from Japan may run a car assembly plant in Canada, for example.

A key insight for managers trying to inspire people across cultures, and trying to understand their diverse mindsets, comes from Clotaire Rapaille, who wrote the bestselling book, *The Culture Code*. Rapaille teaches us that the biggest mistake that we can make is to assume that a range of people viewing the exact same thing will process it in the same way, or will even come to similar conclusions. The culture code is: 'The unconscious meaning we apply to any given thing – a car, a type of food, a relationship, even a country – via the culture we are raised in'.[2] This code is imprinted on us at an early age (usually by the age of seven).

Rapaille shares the story about research he did in France and the US on cheese. He noted that the culture code for cheese in France is 'alive'. The French appreciate that bacteria break down the cheese, giving it interesting smells and flavours. They buy it at room temperature and store it in a cloche (a dome with holes in to keep the flies out but let the air in). Americans, on the other hand, want their cheese 'dead'. They want it pasteurized, wrapped in airtight plastic and preserved – as Rapaille puts it – in a 'morgue' (i.e. the refrigerator).

If the culture code for something as simple as cheese can be so widely divergent, it becomes obvious that managers trying to manage employees from different cultures will need to spend time trying to understand some of their employees' most basic culture codes.

Running glossary

shared objectives
objectives that come from a process
of identifying divergent objectives and
translating them into agreed priorities
and common ground

Managing relationships with people in other departments or companies

One of the trickiest parts of management is that you may often be responsible for the outcomes of projects that are collaborations with other departments, suppliers or even other companies. In these cases, you may be accountable, but you may not have direct management authority over many of the people involved in the outcome: they may report to someone else.

To complicate things further, different departments and different companies may have different goals in mind for completing the project. For example, you may be in charge of a project to redesign a group of retail outlets. The operations team may be primarily concerned with the ergonomics of the workplace. Your marketing team may be primarily concerned with making the store's appearance communicate the brand's identity. Yet your architectural firm may be secretly obsessed with winning a design award by doing something avant-garde.

In these 'shared management' situations, it is vital to establish **shared objectives**. The key is to spend the time upfront to pull the teams together, especially the key managers, to identify divergent objectives and to discuss whether they can all be met and, if not, which ones will take priority. This is a search for common ground. Once the shared objectives have been agreed, each manager then needs to communicate the goals to every employee who will touch the project.

Done right, a manager who is ultimately accountable for a shared-responsibility project does not need to manage everyone who touches the project. Rather, they need to tightly manage the process to ensure cohesive collaboration through a shared vision of what needs to be achieved.

‹ Managing across cultures
Communicate, communicate, communicate
› Productivity tools

Employees do the best when they know the most. They feel most secure when they know what is expected of them. They cannot guess what management would like them to do, nor can they intuit how expectations may change from day to day unless they are told. Communication is vital, and it needs to be regular and consistent at every level.

In larger companies, this calls for a well-thought-out and well-executed internal communications plan. A solid internal communications plan takes into account company-wide, department-level and one-to-one (boss–employee) communication.

A good internal communications plan identifies the stakeholders who need to be communicated with, finds the best strategies for reaching each group, and regularly measures whether or not they received the message.

Petrobras: internal communications

Petrobras, Brazil's national energy company, has over 75,000 employees. One way they communicate to such a large group is through the Petrobras Portal intranet. This internal media allows them to highlight items that are critical to their culture, values, objectives and strategies in a great degree of depth. These stories are then used as part of internal communications for divisions, groups and departments.

For the wider community, such as investors, clients, partners and NGOs, they also produce a print and online magazine. In the image below, the company is emphasizing that concern for the environment needs to be inherent in the decisions made throughout the company. This combination of internal and external communication helps to ensure that concern for the environment is seen in division, group, and department decision making, as well as corporate.

Petrobras Magazine

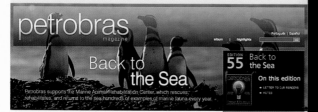

Weekly status meetings

Most managers need to communicate corporate values and objectives to their direct reports, which is usually a manageable group of people (say, five to 50 people), and to communicate from their direct reports upwards through the management chain. Internal communication only works well if it goes both ways!

One of the best ways to open the lines of communication is to hold weekly status meetings. Status meetings are a good business practice to begin with.

They allow employees to report on the progress of their projects, they allow everyone to see what the other members of the group are doing, and they allow the manager to see which projects are succeeding and which ones need help. Over time, they enable the manager to monitor employees' performance.

Beyond the basic business function, however, weekly status meetings allow people to talk. They allow managers to communicate values and goals, and they allow employees to express excitement or concerns. They are the business equivalent of the traditional town hall meeting.

Organizational silence

Many managers have an open-door policy. They may pride themselves on the fact that their employees speak up in meetings. And they may have a strong sense that they know what's on their employees' minds. However, these managers still need to beware of complacency. The *Harvard Business Review* has been researching organizational silence for over a decade. They have found a number of myths that managers tend to abide by. Here are two of the key ones:

If employees are talking openly to me, they are not holding anything back

Forty-two per cent of employees speak up periodically, but also hold back when they feel they have nothing to gain, or something to lose, by doing so.

The only issues that employees are scared to raise involve serious allegations about illegal or unethical activities

Almost 20% of employees fear consequences leading them to withhold information on ordinary problems and improvements.[3]

These myths underscore that managers should not assume that they are making decisions with all the information in hand. Managers need to assume that there are things they do not know, and work hard to make employees feel as comfortable as possible about sharing important information.

Productivity tools

Getting the right talent together and improving communication are critical to market success. Great people all working to the same goals in a constructive environment leads to great efficiency.

Any number of processes or tools can also lead to increased efficiency and allow each person involved in a project to focus on their specific task. Often, when employees are not entirely sure where their task ends and another employee's begins, you will either find two employees trying to do the same task (which is a waste of human resources), or no one doing a task that needs to be done (which is a waste of time).

One simple remedy is for every member of your team to have a detailed job description. Job descriptions are helpful in many ways. They help people to focus on the skills needed when hiring for a specific job; they make sure that new employees know exactly what is expected of them; and they help to avoid job overlap or confusion about who does what.

Another tool that helps each team member focus on their specific tasks is RASCI. This is one of several available tools that identify specific roles in a project, and who does what within it. RASCI is an acronym describing the categories that different people fall into for each project, as follows:

Responsible (R)
This person (usually a single person) is the overall project manager who will be held accountable for the project's success.

Approve (A)
This is the person or people who will approve the key steps.

Support (S)
These are the people (usually many) who will do the work and report to the person responsible for the project.

Consult (C)
These are the people who will be consulted because they have special knowledge that will be useful to the project.

Inform (I)
These are the people who will be kept informed at key stages.

By having detailed job descriptions and by using any number of project management tools, such as RASCI, managers can be more confident that their employees are being productive and that they are focused on their tasks, thus avoiding double-work and work 'gaps'.

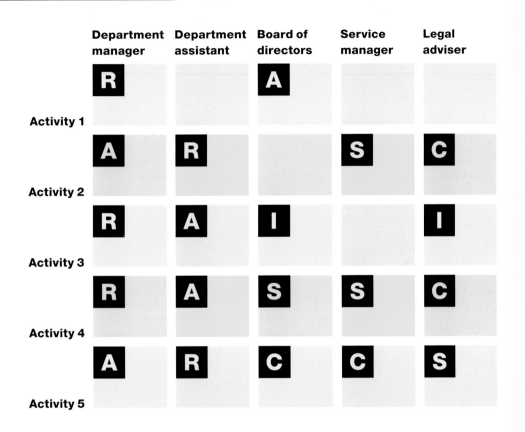

	Department manager	Department assistant	Board of directors	Service manager	Legal adviser
Activity 1	R		A		
Activity 2	A	R		S	C
Activity 3	R	A	I		I
Activity 4	R	A	S	S	C
Activity 5	A	R	C	C	S

Typical RASCI chart

Typical RASCI chart
RASCI is a simple approach that helps ensure that everyone involved in a project recognizes and understands their distinct role within it. As seen on this chart, one employee may have different roles and responsibilities on different projects.

Managing conflict

You can follow every suggestion in this chapter, but you will not be able to completely avoid human nature. You can help to minimize conflicts, but they *will* happen. Likewise, politics and the abuse of power will occur at times, too. A key test for a manager is how he or she reacts when conflict does occur.

What to avoid

Susan Heathfield, a Human Resources (HR) expert who writes on HR issues for www.about.com, offers managers some sound advice about dealing with conflict, detailed in the following paragraphs.

Do not avoid the conflict, hoping it will go away

'It won't. Even if the conflict appears to have been superficially put to rest, it will rear its ugly head whenever stress increases or a new disagreement occurs. An unresolved conflict or interpersonal disagreement festers just under the surface in your work environment. It resurfaces whenever enabled, and always at the worst possible moment. "This, too, shall pass" is not an option – ever.

Do not meet separately with people involved in conflict

'If you allow each individual to tell their story to you, you risk polarizing their positions. The person in conflict has a vested interest in making himself or herself 'right' if you place yourself in the position of judge and jury. The sole goal of the employee, in this situation, is to convince you of the merits of their case.

Do not believe the only people who are affected by the conflict are the participants

'Everyone in your office, and every employee with whom the conflicting employees interact, is affected by the stress. People feel as if they are walking on egg shells in the presence of the antagonists. This contributes to the creation of a hostile work environment for other employees. In the worst case scenario, your organization members take sides and your organization is divided.' **4**

Effective strategies

Once you have identified a problem and decided that it must be dealt with, the question becomes: 'How do I deal with it?' There are a number of strategies that can be employed, depending on the situation.

Collaboration

Asking the conflicting parties to work together on a solution. This works well if there is an adequate level of trust and respect between the two people.

Compromise

Asking each party to give up something and gain something by finding a middle ground.

Competition

Making it a 'winner takes all' proposition. This can be done, for example, by testing one person's plan versus the other or by asking the other employees to take a vote. This works well in highly competitive work environments or when the conflict is about diametrically opposed ideas.

Accommodation

This describes a situation where one party surrenders to end the conflict and maintain the relationship. This works well when one side is far less attached to their point of view or the outcome than the other.[5]

It is important to understand that conflict does not always lead to negative outcomes. Effective conflict management can not only end the conflict without severing relationships, it can also lead to growth and innovation....

Sufyan Baksh-Mohammed
University of Scranton

Good managers need to figure out which strategy is right for which conflict. Part of the decision should depend on which will work best taking into consideration the personalities of the conflicting parties, the degree of conflict and the importance of the issue. An equal part of the decision depends on which outcome is best for the company and its culture.

Above all, managers must avoid the tendency to see all conflict as inherently bad. Some level of conflict is good. Conflict can lead to important discussions about where the organization is going or lead to innovative solutions to seemingly insurmountable problems. Conflict can lead to creativity. But conflict can only lead to creativity if it is brought out in the open and handled appropriately. Always have an open mind!

Managing creative people
> Case study: Bob Seelert and Kayser-Roth

Our brains have two hemispheres: the right and the left. People tend to process information using the dominant side of their brain.

The left side of the brain processes information in a linear manner; placing things in a logical order. Left-brain thinkers tend to take the pieces of information and build them into a whole picture in an ordered process. The right side is more intuitive and spontaneous. Right-brain thinkers have been described as more 'creative' due to their increased ability to think laterally and to develop outside-the-box thoughts or ideas. Right-brain thinkers tend to start with the whole picture and then break it into component parts, using a more random approach.

Most companies are built around left-brain work flow. Planning, timetables, process, order, logic and linear-thinking are prized. Those who master the process are rewarded.

Marketing is a little different, however. Although much of marketing is process-driven, creative communications ideas are a must to emotionally engage customers and to create the kind of lighthouse brands and lovemarks we discussed in Chapter 4.

Advertising agencies, for example, have entire departments of people who carry the title – and are expected to be – 'creative'. Whether they are art directors, photographers, copywriters or graphic designers, all are expected to generate new, non-linear ideas for their companies and clients, every day.

Flexible processes that encourage creativity

Marketing managers have a special challenge that bankers, for example, do not. They need to create strong processes that increase productivity and avoid chaos; but they must also create the flexibility that creative people need to avoid being constrained by processes that work against their natural inclination to take a more intuitive approach.

Having spent 25 years working in the advertising business, I have some suggestions to help organizations enable creative people to be creative. The following suggestions are not just about being nice or letting creative people 'have their way'. They are about understanding how to get the most productivity out of your creative people. They are necessary because marketing companies have asked creative people to do something fundamentally different from other employees. To use excessive process, order and logic in managing creative ideas is counter-productive; it can handcuff the process and stifle the best ideas.

Support

Creative people can be infuriating for rank-and-file employees. Linear, left-brain thinkers often cannot understand why creative people are late for meetings, miss deadlines or misplace important documents. To them, the behaviour of creative people can verge on being unprofessional. When management gives creative people special consideration, petty jealousies can develop.

Marketing managers, therefore, have to walk a fine line. But creative employees need support. Other employees need to be educated about the unique process that leads to creative communications ideas versus more process-oriented work. They need to recognize that the impact of one great creative idea can be many times greater than the impact of other day-to-day work.

Tact

Creatives are far more emotionally involved in their work output. When a photographer presents a photo for approval, or a copywriter presents a script, it represents their deepest ideas and aesthetic standards. Unlike a statistical business report, response to their work elicits highly subjective responses. Those responses can vary from: 'It's beautiful' or 'I love it' to 'It's confusing' or just 'Yuck!'.

Good marketing managers are sensitive to the plight of their creative employees. They protect them from the emotional lows associated with negative feedback.

This does not mean pretending to like their work when it is off-strategy or just plain wrong for your business. It means finding ways to give feedback that are gentle and not hurtful. For example, telling a director what you like about his film first and then pointing out the things that are inconsistent with your goals is far more effective than just saying, 'it's wrong'.

Time

Creative people tend to have trouble sticking to deadlines for two main reasons. One reason is that right-brain thinkers tend to flit from one thing to another. Because they connect ideas in a non-linear way, they like to jump back and forth between thoughts and work assignments. This takes longer, but it increases their ability to be creative. Another reason is that they are more emotionally connected to the work outcome. To them, the work product is not a report that needs to be handed in on time; it is an idea or work of art that will be done when it is great.

A good marketing manager understands and respects this. They give the creative people the extended time that they need in the beginning and are flexible if the creative person asks for 'a few more days'. As creatives like to say: 'No wine before its time.'

Case study: Bob Seelert and Kayser-Roth

I have admired Saatchi & Saatchi chairman Bob Seelert for years. He is a paragon of intelligence, level-headedness, grace and tact. When Seelert was hired to turn around Kayser-Roth, a leading US manufacturer of leg wear, he realized that the employees of the company were very concerned about the future and needed real leadership. We can learn a lot about people management from how Bob faced-up to the situation.

Here is Bob's story of how he managed their concerns, employee by employee:

'When your company is owned by investment bankers and is in a turnaround situation, it is a tense time for employees. They know that things will be different, it will be a demanding period, and there will be a transaction with attendant uncertainty at the end of the deal. Such was the environment I faced at Kayser-Roth….

'On my first day with the company, I addressed the entire headquarters group. I introduced myself, offered my perspective on the current situation and laid out a road map showing how we would proceed. This was a good start, but I wanted to get closer to everyone in the company. Having run a number of different organizations, I knew the best way to learn about an enterprise was to get to know its employees.

'So we launched "Breakfast with Bob" – a programme whereby I would have breakfast with 400 people, pretty close to every employee at headquarters.

'At a rate of seven people at a time, twice a week, I met with everyone in only 29 weeks. Given that most people had never even met the President and CEO, let alone had a one-hour breakfast with him, it was unprecedented.

'It gave me an opportunity to learn a lot about the company, to create an open dialogue that broke down barriers and to put on the table what we needed to do together….

'We opened [each breakfast] by going around the table, introducing ourselves, explaining what we did, how long we had been with the company and telling stories about our personal lives. I always started it off. On the personal side, I'd usually talk about my wife, our three sons, our pet cat and our interests in travel and gardening.

'We all had pads and pencils and I would ask three questions…. What do you like most about the company? What is the single most important thing you would like to see change? What is the one thing we could do differently to help you do your job better?

'I would ask for a volunteer to start and move the discussion along through all three topics, ensuring that we got everyone to participate.

'I learned that the employees really liked working at Kayser-Roth. They were proud of the quality products the company manufactured. Recently, however, they had been poorly led, there had been many shifts in strategy and there was a general inability to achieve excellence in execution. People knew the company had to change, and they were up for it….

'Most of the ideas for improvement centred on the need to improve communications, reduce bureaucracy and increase speed of decision making.

'We ended the sessions with me giving the group an opportunity to ask anything they wanted about me, about the company, about the owners or anything at all. I even got the inevitable 'boxers or briefs?'. The most frequently asked questions centred on the implications of investment bank ownership and what was likely to happen. I answered every question as best as I could.

'At the end, each participant was given a "Bob had breakfast with me" coffee mug. Seven months later, everyone in the company had one.

'This organization-wide activity created an environment where every employee felt like a valued colleague who was being asked to contribute to, and be part of, the solutions we needed to become a successful company. It broke down boundaries, cut through layers and built an open dialogue.'

Question 1
Having breakfast together is one solution for engaging a large group of employees. Can you think of any others?

Question 2
Take a look at the three questions that Bob asked each employee at breakfast. Would you ask the same questions or different ones?

Question 3
Do you think the 'Bob had breakfast with me' mugs served an important purpose?

Every person in your organization is important to its success. When you're the leader, spend quality time with your people to stay connected.

Bob Seelert
Chairman
Saatchi & Saatchi

Is it necessary for a manager, or a CEO, who supervises over 400 people to meet each of them personally, answer their questions and get their input? Bob Seelert would say: 'Yes!'.

Questions and exercises

>

Discussion questions

1

Do you think that there are any parallels between managing a marketing department and coaching a sports team? What, specifically?

2

Have you ever been part of an organization or club that has a strong culture? How did it make you feel to be part of that culture? Did you behave differently? Did you achieve things that you had not expected to?

3

If you had to choose between strategies that supported Skinner (i.e. reinforcing behaviour through tangible reward, punishment and so on) or Freud (i.e. trying to understand and appeal to people's deep-seated emotional needs), which would you choose?

Exercises

1

The next time that you need to work on a group project, use the RASCI system to identify specific roles. Discuss whether it helped to make the project run more smoothly.

2

Imagine that you are hiring someone to be a strategic planner for your team. List three words to describe the person you are looking to hire. Create two specific interview questions to help you identify such a person.

3

List three of your personal values that you would want to instil in any group of employees that would work for you in the future.

Suggested further reading

Jugenheimer, D. W. and L. D. Kelley. (2009). *Advertising Management.* (New York: M. E. Sharpe, Inc.)

Seelert, B. (2009). *Start with the Answer: And Other Wisdom for Aspiring Managers.* (New Jersey: John Wiley & Sons.)

Summary

Managing people goes beyond setting the course, vision or mission. It entails inspiring people in small ways, every day, and managing conflict in a constructive way that builds a sense of shared values. Ultimately, it is about culture creation.

In order to manage people effectively, managers need to have a grasp of basic human psychology to help them understand why people do the things they do, and how to turn negative impulses into positive ones.

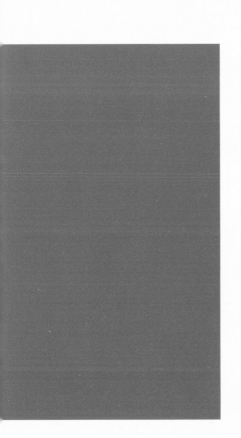

This chapter takes a look at crisis management. Times of crisis test companies and managers. They lay bare whether the company, and the people who run it, are true to all the basics of management that we have reviewed so far in this book. In other words, do they have a clear vision and mission to help them to successfully navigate a crisis? Do they have a strategy in case of crisis? Do they have a brand identity strong enough to overcome the crisis? Do they know how to inspire their people in times of adversity?

We will review the importance of having a crisis management plan, the importance of honest, open communications and of knowing the different requirements of different communications stages, as well as the unique challenges posed by social media. The chapter ends with a case study of a landmark crisis management success story: the Tylenol response to the 1982 product-poisoning scare.

It is amazing how many companies do not have a concrete plan about what to do in case of a crisis. So, rule number one is: you need to have a plan. The most important parts of the plan outline the decision-making process and the communications hierarchy. It is critical that the entire organization know who will be making the key decisions (and who will not) during a crisis and who will be speaking publicly to the media on behalf of the company.

A similar problem arises for companies that have a plan but do not regularly refresh their memory about what it says. If a plan was written three years ago and put on the shelf, it is a safe bet that most managers do not remember exactly what it says. It is a safer bet that anyone who joined the company in the last three years has no clue whatsoever. Companies need to review their strategy at least every year, because a crisis can happen at any time. Having a plan increases the company's speed at dealing with a crisis. And when a crisis rears its ugly head, speed is crucial.

Even companies that are famous for planning can have trouble. In 1999, for example, when Coca-Cola recalled 15 million bottles and cans of their product in Belgium, France, Luxembourg and the Netherlands due to reports of sickness and an unusual taste and odour in their product, they were slow on the uptake. As one report on the crisis put it:

'When the crisis began, company executives took several days to make the matter a top priority. The company did identify and publicly admit that there had been manufacturing mistakes. However, according to some observers, Coca-Cola stumbled repeatedly; exacerbating the situation. For example, an apology to consumers came more than a week after the first public reports of illness. It took ten days after the first child became dizzy and nauseous for top executives to arrive in Belgium and Coca-Cola's initial response attempted to minimize the number and severity of the illnesses.' [1]

A senior Coca-Cola official subsequently stated that the company was not prepared for a crisis of this magnitude and that the situation had been mishandled. A spokesman for the company said: 'The recall was a humbling experience – a wake-up call…'. As this example demonstrates, the bigger and more complex the company, the greater the need for a crisis management plan that is regularly refreshed in your company's memory.

Do not underestimate the impact

In Chapter 2, we introduced General Electric's former chairman and, CEO Jack Welch. In his many years at the helm of GE, he learned a lot about crisis management.

In his 2005 book, entitled *Winning*, he describes reprising a crisis at the GE factory in Valley Forge, Pennsylvania. At the time, he underestimated the importance of time-card irregularities at the factory, which produced missile cones for the US government.
In the end, there was a massive government investigation and GE had to plead guilty to a major fraud by its managers.[2]

Welch noted that crises rarely explode in a single event. Most often they emerge in 'fits and starts'. From his experiences, he outlined five assumptions that all managers should keep in mind when facing a crisis:

> The most challenging part of crisis communication management is reacting – with the right response – quickly. This is because behaviour always precedes communication.

James Lukaszewski
Fellow
Public Relations Society of America

1
The crisis is probably worse than it appears
It helps to assume the worst: that your company was wrong and that you need to fix the problem right away.

2
There are no secrets
Everyone will eventually find out exactly what went on. From day one, absolute transparency should be the rule.

3
Your handling of the situation will probably be portrayed in the worst light
Visibility is critical. State your position openly and honestly from the outset. The truth will be revealed over time.

4
There must be changes in people and process
Real crises call for real changes. Things need to be done differently and often you need new people to do them. Your plans need to rise above rhetoric. Real actions and changes must follow your words. Unfortunately, few crises end without some 'blood on the floor'.

5
Your organization will be stronger, and better, in the end
After a crisis is over, there is a tendency to want to draw a line under it and move on as quickly as possible. Resist this temptation and use the crisis for all it's worth. Teach its lessons every chance you get.

⟨ Have a plan!
Transparency
⟩ Social media and crisis management

This chapter covers a number of key rules for handling a crisis. None are as important as transparency – open and honest communication with customers, media, employees, government and all stakeholders.

Corporate crises are a time when your company and its management need to prove their integrity. A crisis handled well can reinforce an existing reputation for integrity for decades. A crisis mishandled can destroy a company's reputation for integrity within a few weeks or months.

Goodwill

A company's reputation is often called **goodwill**. Goodwill is not just a nice thing to have: when companies are sold, their goodwill value is often carried as a financial asset on the balance sheet. This is the value of the company above and beyond its actual assets. In cases such as IBM or Microsoft, the value of goodwill can be in the billions of dollars (see page 85).

Building goodwill is a key goal of public relations (PR). Most companies conduct PR programmes on an ongoing basis, but they are most important during a crisis.

Marketing managers would do well to remember what the primary goal of all PR programmes is, whether during a crisis or not. The most elegant articulation I have come across about the relationship between PR and goodwill is:

'A public relations programme that is tuned to creating goodwill operates as the conscience of the organization. Creating goodwill demands that both public relations professionals and the clients they represent act with integrity.'[4]

Crises are not a time for a marketing mindset (about selling). It is about a PR mindset (about truth-telling). This is doubly important because in many companies, PR reports into the head of marketing. PR professionals understand the importance of transparency in a way that most other marketing professionals usually do not. They are invaluable assets during a crisis.

Howard Rubenstein, an elder statesman in the PR industry who founded the Rubenstein agency, keeps an instructive paperweight on his desk that says: 'If you tell the truth, you don't have to remember anything.'[5]

Seven steps

James Lukaszewski, a fellow at the Public Relations Society of America, identified a seven-step process for crisis communications, outlined in the table opposite.[6] It is important to know exactly what communications step you are in when communicating information to the public, the press and employees.

Running glossary

goodwill
the market value of a brand above and beyond its assets due to consumers' positive feelings and respect for it

Step	Description	Examples
Candour	Outward recognition of the problem through promptly verbalized public acknowledgement.	'It's our fault.' Answering all questions.
Explanation	Promptly and briefly explain why the problem occurred and know reasons or behaviours that led to the situation.	Finding out the truth. Talking to the victims and their families.
Declaration	A public commitment and discussion of specific, positive steps to conclusively address the issues and resolve the situation.	Being explicit about actions. Avoiding disingenuous phrases like '…if we had only known…' or '… unfortunately, these things happen…'
Contrition	The continuing verbalization of regret, empathy, sympathy, even embarrassment.	Talk and act like someone that you care about has been hurt. Use empathetic language.
Consultation	Promptly ask for help and counsel from the victims, government and the community of origin – even from opponents.	Announce an unassailable panel of independent experts to study, recommend and report publicly.
Commitment	Publicly set organizational goals at zero: zero defects, zero errors, etc.	Establish a permanent, broadly representative advisory group.
Restitution	Find a way to quickly pay the price.	Exceed community expectations (e.g. immediately set up an independently administered fund to cover short- and long-term victim expenses).

James Lukaszewski's seven step process for crisis management

Social media and crisis management

The emergence of online social media as a popular way for people to interact, and for organizations to market products, has increased the speed with which a crisis can spread, as well as the speed with which it can be resolved. Domino's Pizza, for example, which has franchises in over 60 countries worldwide, found out how quickly social media can incite a crisis. In April 2009, two bored Domino's employees posted a video to YouTube showing them engaging in a number of unsanitary acts with Domino's food, including one employee sticking cheese up his nose and including it in a sandwich intended for a customer.

Seemingly in an instant, Domino's reputation was tarnished, worldwide, before many in their Michigan headquarters even knew what was happening. Such is the breadth and speed of social media. Between 13–17 April, negative blog-post mentions of Domino's on the web increased tenfold.

The lighter side of crisis management
This cartoon underscores the first rule of crisis management: don't panic!

>

When you have a crisis, the crisis itself becomes one of your biggest assets if that crisis is bad enough. Everyone gets very modest and humble and listens. If you need to do rough things, you do rough things.

Carl-Henric Svanberg
CEO
Ericsson

But Domino's executives reacted relatively quickly. Within 48 hours, Domino's posted their own YouTube video featuring the brand's president. They also had their social media team communicating regularly on Twitter and with relevant websites.

The company has been criticized for not doing more in the first 24 hours, but within that time they communicated to all their franchisees, identified the culprits, fired them, handed them over to the police and had the store inspected by the health department. They hardly frittered the time away. They got their house in order first, so that their communications would have real meaning.

"The Crisis Management Seminar broke up early. The speaker got a paper cut and flipped out"

Some people need to see everything that you are doing in real time

In McIntyre's words: 'If there is a crisis happening in the social media realm… there is a segment of the population that wants you to put on a microphone and a webcam and describe what you are doing as you do it.'

You need to keep track of social media constantly, not just when there is a crisis

Domino's now looks at a chart showing online buzz every day.

Don't panic

Companies successfully handle thousands of complex things every day. Make the crisis one of them. For people in marketing or communications, you are the communications leaders. You cannot panic or everyone else will too.[7]

Lessons learned

Looking for lessons about social media and crisis management, Domino's vice president of communications, Tim McIntyre, focused on the following:

It can be easy to underestimate social pass-along value online and the subsequent traditional media interest that comes from it

Domino's did not anticipate what he called the 'man, you've got to see this' factor. Nor did they anticipate the 'sheer explosion' of interest from traditional news media.

< Social media and crisis management
Case study: Tylenol versus Cadbury
> Questions and exercises

Unfortunately, most case studies in crisis management are examples of companies that have got it wrong. It is always easy, after the fact, to see what companies could have done right. One example of a company that got it right from the start is Johnson & Johnson's (J&J) handling of the Tylenol (pain relief medication) scare in 1982.

The way in which J&J handled the recall now represents the gold standard for crisis management. It started when someone injected cyanide into some bottles that were already on the shelf in Chicago, ultimately killing seven people. The tampering was the top story on all news channels and Tylenol saw its market share drop from 37% to less than 7%.

The immediate question for J&J management was what they should do. Since the product had been tampered with after it left the factory, they were not strictly responsible and there was nothing wrong with the product itself. Also, as Patrick Murphy, professor of ethics at the University of Notre Dame, noted: 'Their legal counsel and, from what I have heard, the FBI as well, said maybe you shouldn't recall this product because this will make it look like some crazy person could bring a major corporation to its knees.'

James Burke, chairman of J&J, made a swift decision. He looked at his company's credo, which had been written by the company's founder, Robert Wood Johnson. The first sentence of the credo states: 'We believe our first responsibility is to doctors, nurses and patients, to mothers, fathers and all others who use our products and services.' Burke decided that the company's credo dictated protecting people first and protecting the product second. He ordered an immediate recall of all Tylenol products nationwide. The recall amounted to over 30 million bottles, and cost J&J over £63 million ($100 million).

The company pulled advertising for Tylenol, issued media alerts, held press conferences, created a helpline number for consumers to call; Burke even appeared on top television programmes such as *60 Minutes*. Today, these approaches are common; at the time they were unparalleled.

J&J introduced new triple-seal, tamper-resistant packaging, offered price discounts, gave over 2,000 presentations to the medical community, and aggressively relaunched the product with a new advertising campaign. The result: Tylenol quickly regained its share and market leadership, even in the face of another tampering scare in 1986. Perhaps the most important lesson for J&J was to stay true to its credo, even in challenging times.

Cadbury

Let's compare Tylenol's approach to that of Cadbury, one of the world's largest confectionery companies, when they had to recall seven of their branded products due to salmonella contamination in June 2006. The confectioneries were contaminated when dirty water leaking from a pipe splashed on to a conveyor belt at their Herefordshire factory in the UK. Cadbury learned about the possible contamination in January 2006, but failed to inform health authorities.

The contamination was not reported to the UK Food Standards Agency (FSA) until June 2006, a full five months later. Only then, after being lambasted by the media and the FSA, did Cadbury recall the products. Cadbury's reason for not immediately bringing the contamination to the attention of the FSA sounded logical. As a Cadbury spokesman put it: 'The levels [of contamination] are significantly below the standard that would be any health problem.' They noted that their tests were far more stringent than anyone else's, and so were able to pick up minute traces. The levels found, they said, were significantly below the level needed to cause even a mild stomach upset. They were 'absolutely satisfied' that their products were safe to eat.

Cadbury's assertions sounded logical, but they contradicted the statement that bacteriologist Professor Hugh Pennington of Aberdeen University made to the BBC that the only safe level of salmonella in chocolate was 'zero'.

Cadbury's management failed to see that the question was not whether the contamination was significant or minute. The question was whether consumers could implicitly trust Cadbury to put their well-being first and the company's well-being second, as J&J had done. Cadbury failed this test.

An examination of the Cadbury recall case in *Corporate Reputational Review* stated: 'Cadbury's crisis management strategy to the food poisoning was counter-intuitive to the traditional crisis management mantra of being open, honest and responsive.'[8]

When a corporate crisis happens, crisis management strategy should be simple and straightforward. The watchwords are 'speed' and 'transparency'. The focus is on protecting consumers' and society's interests first and the economic impact to your company and brand second.

Question 1
How are a company's handling of a crisis and its mission statement related, as seen in the Tylenol case?

Question 2
How important was executive leadership in the Tylenol recall? Was there any comparable executive visibility or leadership at Cadbury?

Questions and exercises

Discussion questions

1

If it is a bad idea to underestimate a crisis, can it be just as bad to overestimate one? If so, when?

2

If you were a marketing director and you had just been informed of a crisis by email, what is the first thing that you would do?

3

Do crisis management plans always need to include social media approaches, or just sometimes?

Exercises

1

Break into two teams. Pretend that you are the management team for an airline. Your job is to create a crisis management plan in case of a plane crash. Develop the plans in your separate teams, then compare and debate them.

2

Read up on BP's handling of the oil spill crisis in the Gulf of Mexico in 2010. Make a list of all the things that they did right and what you would have done better.

3

Visit Cadbury's website and the website of their new parent company, Kraft Foods. What are their missions or product philosophies? Debate whether they could have been inspired by these to do a better job on the recall?

Summary

Crises are the times when managers prove their ultimate worth. Although every crisis is unique, many of the issues that need to be handled in a crisis can be planned ahead (for example, who will speak for the company to the media during the crisis?). When a company has a strong sense of what it is, and what it is about, and combines that with clear plans about what to do in the case of a crisis – any crisis – then its managers have an excellent chance of weathering stormy seas. In some situations, a crisis handled with skill can actually leave a brand better off than it was before the crisis happened.

Suggested further reading

Carroll, C. (Spring 2009) Defying a Reputational Crisis — Cadbury's Salmonella Scare: Why are Customers Willing to Forgive and Forget? *Corporate Reputational Review*, 12, pp. 64–82.

Marconi, J. (1997) *Crisis Management: When Bad Things Happen to Good Companies*. (Chicago: NTC Business Books)

Welch, J. and S. Welch. (2005) *Winning*. (New York: HarperCollins)

This chapter looks at business numbers. Some numbers, such as sales numbers, are very straightforward and need not be covered in this book. Other numbers are about relationships. These are slightly more complex and are important for managers to master, so they are covered here.

Numerical relationships in business fall into a number of distinct categories. Two of the most important are financial numerical relationships, known as 'financials', and analytical numerical relationships, known as 'analytics'.

Financial measures tell us about the fiscal health of the company overall, while analytical measures tell us how successful our business programmes are at building our business. We will look at some of the most important relationships and rules in each area. And we will see how managers who have a great grasp for these relationships, people like WPP chief executive Martin Sorrell and Optimedia CEO Antony Young, use them to gain competitive advantage.

Accounting is the method by which companies categorize their income, their expenditures, their assets and their liabilities. Accountants summarize these for company management (and stockholders) using two basic instruments: the *income statement* and the *balance sheet*. The income statement lists a company's total income and subtracts total expenses, showing a net profit or loss at the bottom. It answers the question: 'How much money did we make?'. The balance sheet lists all company **assets** and **liabilities**. It is called a balance sheet because a company's assets and liabilities are always equal to each other, or in balance. It answers the question: 'How much do we own and owe?'.

Assets and liabilities in perpetual balance can be a somewhat confusing thought. It is easy to observe that companies often have millions (sometimes even billions) of dollars worth of factories, orders and cash. It is not necessarily intuitive that they must be in debt to the exact same amount. This is especially confusing if we think that many companies make money every year, so surely profits must lead to assets above and beyond what the companies owe?

The answer to this conundrum is investors and lenders. Everything a company buys, and everything a company makes above and beyond what it owes to suppliers for materials and so on, is ultimately the property of its investors. Those investors may be stockholders, partners or proprietors. Therefore, as the company's wealth increases or decreases, it owes either more or less to its investors. In many companies, this debt to owners is the company's single largest liability. It is known as stockholders' equity or owners' equity (i.e. the value of the owners' stake in the company).

Running glossary

assets
property and things of value –
represents how much you *own*

liabilities
financial obligations –
represents how much you *owe*

WPP's Tokyo windfall

How important is a firm understanding of financial details – such as balance sheet valuations – for top managers? Just ask Sir Martin Sorrell, chief executive of WPP group, the world's largest advertising conglomerate, which owns many iconic advertising agencies including J. Walter Thompson (JWT), Ogilvy & Mather (O&M) and Young & Rubicam (Y&R).

In the mid-1980s, Sorrell bought a small supermarket basket manufacturer based in Kent, England, named Wire and Plastic Products (WPP), which he then used as a foundation (called a 'holding company') for aggregating over 100 marketing services brands. In 1987, WPP launched a bid to buy the venerable JWT at $45 per share. They eventually bought the company for $50 per share, a total purchase price of $566 million (£364 million).

At the time, half a billion dollars seemed a very steep price to pay for a company that had recently fallen on hard times. As one Wall Street analyst put it in the late 1980s: 'They [JWT] have problems in places other companies don't even have places.'[1]

Sorrell, however, was a canny investor, whose background was finance rather than advertising. As a man who knew his way around a company balance sheet, he soon discovered that the balance sheet value of some of JWT's assets and the real market value were considerably different. At first, Sorrell and his team were excited about the real value of JWT's London headquarters in Berkeley Square, but that would ultimately pale in comparison to the enormous disparity between the balance sheet valuation and real market value of JWT's Tokyo property.

In 1987, Japan was in the midst of an unprecedented real estate boom. When a bank offered to lend WPP $100 million (£65 million) against the Tokyo property, Sorrell figured it was worth twice that. In the end, WPP bought JWT and quickly sold the Tokyo property for a whopping $205 million (£132 million), more than one third the purchase price of the whole company.

By knowing his way around a balance sheet, Sorrell turned what looked like a gross overpayment into a bargain.

Basic financial formulas

The balance sheet is a particularly useful tool for looking at numerical relationships, which can help managers to judge the financial fitness and competitive health of the company.

While there are dozens of balance sheet measures that companies look at on a regular basis, we will consider a few of the most basic and useful. Before we do, however, we need to differentiate between current and long-term assets, and current and long-term liabilities. Current assets are things such as cash, cash equivalents, money or accounts receivable and inventory. Current assets are known as 'liquid' or 'quick' assets, because they can be immediately spent or translated into cash relatively quickly – usually in less than one year – as opposed to long-term assets.

Some of the most useful financial formulas focus on current assets and liabilities because they help to ascertain the financial health of a company at the present time. They are especially helpful when an unforeseen event forces the company to cover many of its liabilities quickly. In the previous chapter, we discussed crisis management. A key part of crisis management is knowing what kind of financial shape you are in. The 2010 BP oil spill in the Gulf of Mexico is a good example. Oil companies need to know that they are in a position to pay out huge amounts in claims and fines at any moment should there be an oil spill or similar accident.

Three of the best measures of current financial health are working capital, current ratio and the acid test ratio.

1
Working capital

This measure shows a company's ability to pay off its short-term debts and still have money left over to run day-to-day operations. It is calculated simply by subtracting current liabilities from current assets. It is also a good measure of a company's business efficiency (i.e. the ongoing cycle of making sales, collecting payment and paying expenses).

Working capital =
current assets –
current liabilities

2
Current ratio

This is a measure of a company's liquidity (i.e. its ability to bring cash to bear quickly on its current liabilities) in the form of a **ratio**. It is a simple calculation of current assets divided by current liabilities. As an example, if Company X has current assets of £150,000 and current liabilities of £100,000, its current ratio would be £150,000/£100,000 or £1.50, indicating that for every £1 of debt, Company X could muster £1.50 in cash.

Current ratio =
current assets ÷
current liabilities

3
The acid test ratio

This ratio is a harder test of a company's current financial health. It is similar to the current ratio, but it subtracts inventory and prepaid assets from the current asset total in recognition, for example, that inventory is the least liquid of current assets and can be damaged, become obsolete or be stolen. Too much inventory can also be a sign of inefficiency. Looking again at Company X, if current assets are £150,000, inventory is £40,000 and prepaid assets are £20,000, against a current liability base of £100,000, then the acid test ratio would be (£150,000– £40,000–£20,000)/£100,000 or £0.90. Looked at this way, Company X would fall just short of meeting its total short-term debts should they have to do so very quickly.

The acid test ratio =
(current assets –
inventory –
prepaid assets)
÷ current liabilities

In my previous job, our chief financial officer had a favourite saying: 'Cash is reality'. For managers looking at accounting statements, this fact can sometimes be obscured, especially since so many assets are paid for upfront, but accounted for (or 'accrued') over many years. These formulas bring into focus how cash, or cash equivalents, are indeed financial reality, especially in times of crisis.

Running glossary

ratio
the quantitative relation between two amounts showing the number of times that one value contains or is contained within the other

❮ Financial balance sheets and income statements
Basic financial formulas
❯ Dashboards

The rule of 72 and doubling time

		Category	Company A	Company B
Year: 2010	**Sales**	100,000 units	30,000 units	20,000 units
	Share	100%	30%	20%
	Growth rate	—	3%	8%
	Doubling time	—	24 years	9 years
Year: 2019	**Sales**	139,143 units	39,143 units	40,000 units
	Share	100%	28%	29%

The rule of 72

The rule of 72 is one of the most useful 'rule of thumb' measures available to managers. It can be used to quickly measure growth, financial or otherwise. It is a simple formula that helps to calculate the amount of time it will take something to double based on a consistent rate of *compound growth*. The rule of 72 is so useful because it accounts for the compounding effect of the growth rate year after year. If, for example, a company has invested £100,000 at 9% interest, how long will it take for the money to double to £200,000? Easy, it will take eight years, or 72 divided by nine.

Where the rule of 72 is most useful is in measuring relative growth. In the example shown in the chart above, if Company A has 30% market share and is growing at 3%, and Company B has 20% market share and is growing at 8%, then, assuming that the relative growth rates do not change, Company A will double its sales in 24 years, while Company B will do it in only nine years! When those nine years are up, all other things in the category being equal, Company B will actually be bigger in terms of sales and share than Company A.

The rule of 72 =

72 ÷
rate of growth

Analytics and return on investment

One place where financial measures and analytical business measures meet is in measuring return on investment (ROI). At their core, analytical measures are about ascertaining whether specific business programmes are building business, and generating profit (i.e. providing a return on the investment put into them). With the growth of the Internet and our unparalleled ability to use it to generate reams of data about marketing programmes, online sales and so on, analytics and ROI measurement have become something of a Holy Grail in marketing today.

Antony Young, CEO of Optimedia US, a large, integrated media communications company, is an expert in measuring ROI. In his 2007 book, *Profitable Marketing Communications,* he and his co-author Lucy Aitkin outlined some new ways to think about marketing through the lens of ROI measurement:

1

'Think of marketing ROI as another name for "profit"'

Marketing can lead to two types of profit: positive cash flow (i.e. short-term money generation) and asset appreciation (i.e. longer-term sales effects).

2

'Treat the marketing budget as a loan'

In fact, don't use the word 'budget' at all, which implies money there to be spent. Assume it is a loan that must be paid back with interest.

3

'Think of marketing channels as different "ways of making money"'

Television campaigns are usually longer-term investments with big potential payouts, while direct marketing, for example, is like shorter-term deposits with consistent and expected payouts.

Once you have your head in the right place about ROI, you need to create specific measures, or even batteries of measures, for each specific programme. Setting the 'right' metrics is job one, creating a measurement culture (see page 141) is job two.

Marketers are generally good at recommending strategies to spend their budget wisely. Yet the big question for companies is: 'should I be spending at all?'

Antony Young
CEO Optimedia US

Dashboards

⟩ Case study: Samsung – becoming a market leader

Today, digital technology gives us the opportunity to create hundreds, even thousands, of measures for every programme. What managers are learning is that too much information can be as bad – or sometimes worse – than no information. Too much information can lead to what is known as 'paralysis by analysis' (i.e. having too much information, much of it conflicting, is so confusing that it becomes impossible to make clear strategic decisions).

The key to avoiding paralysis is to find a relatively small, manageable set of measures that really matter. My recommendation is that no marketing programme should be focused on more than ten measures. The key is to find the ten (or fewer) measures that really make a difference. These are known as **key performance indicators** (KPIs). KPIs can be such things as measurements of sales, share, customer satisfaction, consumer engagement or productivity; whatever measures are most closely related to the success of the product or service.

Running glossary

key performance indicators (KPIs)
a handful of statistical measures – usually fewer than ten – that are regularly tracked to measure the success of a company, a brand, or a marketing programme

Once you have identified the KPIs, the next step is to compile them on one sheet of paper that will be updated regularly (weekly, monthly or quarterly) to allow you to judge your success and formulate ongoing strategies. Looking at this sheet of paper, which should be pinned up on the office walls and cubicles of every team member, is akin to looking at the dials and displays on your car as you are driving, so it is commonly known in business as a 'dashboard'.

Appearance is also important for dashboards. The easier they are to look at, process and comprehend, the more useful they will be. In fact, simple graphics are vital to successful analytics. Although the people who design the actual measures may need PhDs in statistics, the employees who use the measures every day should find them approachable and simple, not daunting. Many people have an ingrained fear of statistics. A well-conceived dashboard allays these fears.

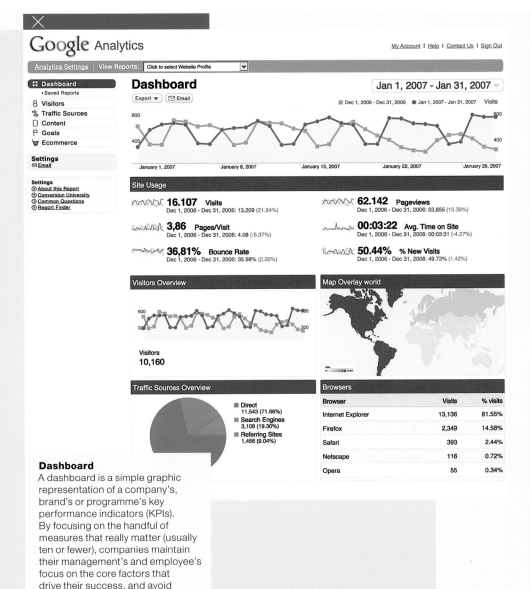

Dashboard

A dashboard is a simple graphic representation of a company's, brand's or programme's key performance indicators (KPIs). By focusing on the handful of measures that really matter (usually ten or fewer), companies maintain their management's and employee's focus on the core factors that drive their success, and avoid decision-making 'paralysis'.

✕

Profile: Avinash Kaushik

When learning about analytics, KPIs and dashboards, one should consider the ideas of one of the leading minds in the field: Avinash Kaushik. Kaushik works for Google. He has the intriguing title of Analytics Evangelist. One of his roles is to help people use the mountains of data churned up by online activity and turn it into something simple and useful. In fact, simplicity is so central to Kaushik's philosophy that his blog is called Occam's Razor, after the principle of the 14th century logician, William of Occam (Ockham), which posited that solutions should not be complicated beyond necessity. Kaushik puts it in more modern parlance: 'The simpler the explanation, the more likely it is better than a complex one.'

In order to increase insightful data while fostering simplicity, Kaushik recommends that dashboards include the following:

Benchmarks

Benchmarks can be both internal (e.g. based on your brand's historical performance or the performance of other brands in your company) and external (e.g. based on industry or competitor performance). They make it immediately clear whether the current measures on the dashboard are signs of success or failure.

Segmenting

Break the results down by relevant marketing segments that you use for targeting (e.g. age, sex or income).

Trending

Current results should be put in the context of previous results (e.g. weekly, quarterly, biannually and annually).

Insights

Use some brief words to help the reader understand the charts and numbers. They may be able to see that sales are up 2% since last quarter, but how good is that? A statement underneath saying 'our best month ever', or 'disappointing!' or 'the largest period-to-period growth in two years', puts the numbers in context for the reader.

Lines of sight to management objectives

When the measures on your dashboard for a marketing programme fall directly in line with company goals and strategies, it is much easier to get top management's attention, support and budget for your programme.

Creating a measurement culture

As we mentioned in Chapter 5, business tools are only as good as management's ability to inspire employees to use them effectively. Regarding analytics, it is about creating a culture that embraces them, even though the word alone may be anathema to statistically challenged employees.

We can learn a lot by considering Kaushik's title: Analytics Evangelist. Analytics is obviously critical to the success of Google. Rather than just call Kaushik an 'analyst', they have asked him to 'evangelize' analytics within the corporation. If the term sounds religious or even fanatical, that is by design. His job is not just to do data analysis, but rather it is to inspire everyone in the organization to do it, do it well and to put data-based decisions – aided by simple analytical tools like dashboards – into practice every day.

Statistics are no substitute for judgement.

Henry Clay
American statesman

Case study: Samsung – becoming a market leader

Writing for the *Harvard Business Review* in 2003, Marcel Corstjens and Jeffrey Merrihue detailed the story of the arrival of Eric Kim as executive vice-president of global marketing at Samsung in 1999. Kim's goal was to transform Samsung's competitive position: to turn it into a market leader rather than the low-cost, low-profile brand it was at the beginning of the 21st century. The stakes were enormous, covering dozens of electronics and hi-tech categories, including phones, PDAs, DVD players, televisions, semiconductors and computer monitors.

Before Kim set out to spend his £700 million ($1 billion) global marketing budget, he focused on improving Samsung's data collection and analysis, which had traditionally been erratic and had been little help in decision making. For example, Samsung could not even compare most marketing data across regions because the information was not standardized. In fact, Samsung had information for fewer than 30% of its country-category combinations.

This was a huge problem for a company that sold products in hundreds of countries worldwide. To solve the problem, Kim focused on three key areas:

1
collecting clear, consistent data points worldwide

2
benchmarking

3
simplifying data sharing

Samsung standardized data collection in different countries, including:

- Total population and population of target buyers
- **Per capita** spending power
- Spending on product categories per capita
- Category penetration
- Category growth
- Brand share
- Media spending
- Previous marketing spending
- Competitor metrics
- Category profitability

Benchmark data was collected to give context to the measures. This allowed Samsung to evaluate various spending and strategy scenarios and to better predict which approaches would yield a higher ROI. All of this information for all of the countries was compiled in a single place: Samsung's marketing intranet site, known as M-Net.

Decisions

Once compiled and analysed, the data exposed a clash between existing investment and potential ROI growth. Three important decisions were made from this analysis:

■ North America and Russia accounted for 45% of the marketing spending, yet both markets offered low comparative growth. Kim and his team decided to cut spending in these markets by 10%.

■ Europe and China, which accounted for 31% of the budget, were higher profit/ROI potential markets, so their budget was increased to 42%.

■ Mobile phones, vacuums and air conditioning products accounted for half the current spending. It was decided that this investment could be decreased by 22% to invest in marketing new products.

Samsung used better collection and analysis of data to reallocate almost £94 million ($150 million) worth of spending to improve ROI.

As we have learned throughout this book, analysis can only go so far in transforming organizations, particularly big organizations like Samsung. Great analysis needs to be combined with great management leadership. That is why Kim and his team conducted over 100 meetings and workshops with marketing staff. These meetings were about getting feedback and improved insight into the findings. They also accomplished broad buy-in among key employee stakeholders to the findings and eventual plans. In countries that were going to receive budget cuts, Kim made sure to present the case in person to avoid any feeling of being slighted in those markets and to make sure that the communication was precise. Kim told the *Harvard Business Review*:

'In a project such as this, there's no substitute for effective communication when it comes to implementing change.... We had to explain what we were doing, and how it was critical to the future success of Samsung globally.'

Running glossary

per capita
for each person; in relation to people taken individually

< Dashboards
Case study: Samsung – becoming a market leader
> Questions and exercises

Old and new approaches

As demonstrated in the table below, this more objective, fact-based, data-driven approach to decision making was dramatically different in comparison to Samsung's traditional approach.[2]

Traditional approach	Fact-based, data-driven approach
Category managers campaign for incrementally larger budgets.	Critical country- and product-category data are collated into M-Net.
Headquarters' (HQ) marketing management responds based on incomplete information, historical approach and gut instinct.	Using M-Net's analytical engines, corporate marketers identify high-potential country-category combinations.
Outsized increases go to the biggest markets and 'squeaky wheels'.	What-if scenarios are tested to determine the most effective allocation of marketing resources.
Over- and under-investments are rampant, yet no one knows where or by how much.	The allocation is refined based on insights of field marketing managers, and then finalized by HQ.
Marketing's total budget appears arbitrary and indefensible.	The fact-based case for the allocation is presented in meetings with field managers.
Top management grows increasingly uncomfortable with the overall marketing investment.	Top management gains confidence in its level of marketing investment.

Samsung's data-driven approach

Samsung: one of the most valuable brands in the world
Eric Kim's arrival as executive vice-president of global marketing in 1999 led to a focus on data-driven marketing decision making. In less than a decade, new analytics approaches and tools, such as the company's marketing intranet, M-Net, helped to propel Samsung from a second-tier bargain brand to one of the world's most valuable brands.

The results

The results have been astounding. Combined with significant increases in product quality and innovation, Samsung's more focused marketing approach has helped power it to become one of the top brands in the world in the past ten years, from its starting point as a tier 2, low-price brand. Within a few years of Kim's arrival, in 2002 and 2003, Samsung was named by Interbrand – which ranks companies based on the value of their brands – the fastest growing brand in the world in terms of brand value. In fact, the value of the Samsung brand doubled from £3.3 billion ($5.2 billion) to £6.9 billion ($10.8 billion) over the three-year period from 2001 to 2003. In 2009, Interbrand announced that Samsung had broken into the top 20 most valuable brands in the world, at number 19.

Question 1
In a company the size of Samsung, why do you think one man in one department was able to incite so much change?

Question 2
What do you think is the relative importance of Kim personally presenting the plans in countries that were to receive budget cuts?

Question 3
Looking at the list of data that Samsung's marketing department collected and standardized, how would you rank them in importance? Would you add or subtract any measures?

Questions and exercises
⟩

Discussion questions

1
Why do you think most companies
look at budgets as money to be spent
rather than as a loan to be repaid…
with interest?

2
Can you think of examples in your own
day-to-day life where Occam's Razor
(i.e. simple solutions outperforming
complex ones) holds true?

3
Imagine that you are the marketing
director for Microsoft Corp.
What measures might you put
on your dashboard?

Exercises

1
Get the annual report for a company
of your choice (most big companies
publish them online). Calculate
their current ratio and acid test ratio.
What do the results tell you?

2
Look up the size of China's current
gross domestic product (GDP) and
current GDP growth rate versus those
of the United States. Assuming that
the current GDP growth rates stay
about the same for each country,
how long (using the rule of 72) will it
take for each economy to double?
How long will it take for China's
economy to be as big as that of
the United States? Is that longer or
shorter than you expected given the
initial difference in their sizes?

3
Break into groups. Each group
should pick a different big, famous
company. Each group should develop
a dashboard based on what they think
are the most important measures for
that company's success. When you
are done, compare them; discuss
how and why they are different.

Summary

Having a firm grasp of numerical relationships is vital in management. You need not be great with numbers, but you need to understand the basic financial and analytical relationships that indicate whether your company is financially sound and whether your product is succeeding in the marketplace. The key is to find simple tools – such as dashboards – that simplify the numerical information, allowing your team to focus on what is important when they are awash in a sea of data.

Suggested further reading

Gowthorpe, C. (2005) *Business Accounting and Finance: For Non-Specialists*. (London: Thompson Learning)

Kaushik, A. (2007) *We Analytics: An Hour a Day*. (Indianapolis: Wiley Publishing)

Young, A. and L. Aitkin. (2007) *Profitable Marketing Communications: A Guide to Marketing Return on Investment*. (London: Kogan Page)

This chapter examines ethical business practice. Ethics go right to the heart of whether companies, and the managers who run them, add value to their employees, their customers and to society at large. We will look at both sides of ethics: ethical practice that is voluntary and driven by conscientiousness, and ethical practice regulated by legislation.

This chapter includes a number of specific suggestions for how individual managers and companies as a whole can be more ethical and legally compliant. It ends with a case study about how two managers at a top advertising agency ignored these factors and consequently paid a very heavy price.

What makes any discussion of ethics so difficult is that any decision can be rationalized. There are two sides to every issue (sometimes more), and often one decision can be made to seem as ethical as another. For example, is charging a client an inflated, above-market rate for work ethical if they don't have an issue with your price? On the one hand, it is 'smart business', on the other it could be considered 'gouging' to charge more for the same work.

In the marketing world, cases of product misrepresentation are not always clear cut. For example, in 1990, Volvo ran afoul of the Federal Trade Commission (FTC) when they made a commercial showing their car being run over by a monster truck without major damage to the roof. It came out later that Volvo had reinforced the roof when shooting the demonstration. This seems like a clear case of poor ethics until you consider that the commercial was based on a real-life monster truck show where, indeed, the Volvo was the only car left uncrushed. To make an ad takes several repeated shots, or 'takes'. In order to stand repeated crushing, Volvo reinforced the roof.

> *Ethics relate to what is good or bad, as defined by moral duties and obligations. Ethics establish a set of rules, based – for the individual – on personal integrity; and – for the organization – on company and industry standards.*
>
> D. W. Jugenheimer and L. D. Kelley
> *Advertising Management*

The fact remains that if you are run over by a monster truck, you are pretty safe in a Volvo. In this light, the company's actions may be seen as more ethical than implied by the FTC judgement, but it remains relative.

Ethical issues often boil down to something we covered in Chapter 1: corporate values. Different companies have different values. Ethical behaviour can often be judged by whether a company has held true to its values. The phrase 'everybody else does it' does not pass for a corporate ethical standard.

It is also worth remembering that ethical problems do not just occur when dealing with customers; they also occur inside companies on a day-to-day basis regarding employee safety, harassment, promotion, discrimination and so on.

The grandmother test

About a year ago, I was teaching a class of graduate students at Syracuse University about business ethics. We did the usual reading, looked at a few case studies and then held a round-table discussion. When I asked the students if they could summarize ethical business in a sentence, one soft-spoken young woman said: 'making a decision that would make your grandmother proud'. In all my years of running companies, working for clients and teaching, I have never heard it put better or more simply. I now talk to students about ethical decisions passing the grandmother test.

Would Grandma approve?

Doing the right thing

General Norman Schwarzkopf, who was commander of coalition forces in the first Gulf war, is relatively 'black and white' in his view about ethical behaviour. He was quoted as saying: 'The truth of the matter is that you always know the *right thing* to *do*. The hard part is *doing* it.' He holds that our knowledge of the right thing to do is innate and the ability to do it, especially in the face of resistance, is the greatest test of leadership, military or otherwise. The fact that Schwarzkopf is famous for leading men into war shows just how nebulous discussions of ethics can become.

Another relevant quote, which I often use when teaching students about business ethics is: 'A principle is only a principle when it costs you money.' This underscores how easy it is to do the right thing when there is no cost to you. The real test of management integrity comes when you have to pay for your principles, either by spending money or losing out on the potential to make more money.

Taken together, these two quotes remind managers to listen to their conscience and to let their conscience outweigh popular opinion and/or monetary self-interest when deciding the right course of action.

Embracing regulation

Legal regulation takes many ethical decisions out of the hands of individual managers and companies. For the protection of consumers and society as a whole, some areas of business are put beyond the reach of ethical subjectivity. Some businesses, such as pharmaceuticals, are heavily regulated. Others, like the cereal industry, are regulated in specific cases, for example, when they market sugary cereals to children. Some industries are very lightly regulated.

In many cases, industries have created self-regulation guidelines to police their behaviour so that the government does not have to. What is regulated, versus what is not regulated, is a function of cultural values, so the severity of regulation in many industries can vary greatly from country to country. In some countries, alcohol and/or cigarette advertising is banned. In others, it may be restricted in specific areas. In others still, they may not be restricted at all. The way in which certain products are sold or presented in a highly religious country, such as Saudi Arabia, is significantly different than it is in a highly liberal country such as Holland.

Compliance

We have said that an ethical culture is important. A culture of *compliance* is just as important. Regulation can only be truly effective when those being regulated choose to comply, especially when compliance is voluntary. Even when it is not voluntary, governments do not always have the resources to go after every company that does not comply with the letter of the law.

To many managers, legal compliance is a bother, which can be seen as limiting their marketing potential. However, corporate cultures that are diligent in compliance often find, by being so, that they are more in tune with their customers. Over time, these companies, by being champions for the protection of consumers, find that they actually win in the marketplace because consumers grow to trust them.

This isn't just a legal compliance issue for us. We consider the privacy issue to be an opportunity to reinforce our brand image.

Tom Warga
Senior vice president and general auditor
New York Life Insurance Co.

Online marketing to children

A case in point is marketing to children over the Internet. The swift growth of digital media and the slower pace of regulation allowed many marketers to side-step existing advertising regulations regarding marketing to children in traditional media, such as television. Governments in countries such as the US, Australia and Canada did finally step in and adapt the Children's Online Privacy Protection Act of 1998 (COPPA) requiring commercial operators of websites to obtain 'verifiable parental consent' before collecting or disclosing personal information about children under 13 years old.

Interestingly, this legislation was based on previously developed self-regulation. The Children's Advertising Review Unit (CARU) of the Council of Better Business Bureaus had already set the rules – which were being followed voluntarily by many companies – that became the basis of COPPA.

According to Wayne Keeley, director of CARU and vice president of the Council of Better Business Bureaus: 'We try to find the common ground between protection of children, which is our uppermost priority, and responsible advertising.' The companies that were already following these guidelines had a big competitive advantage.

Professional marketers realize that compliance is always better for business in the long run. In the case of COPPA, it allowed many companies marketing to children to become society's most ardent advocates for children's rights and protections.

Ten steps to a more ethical and legally compliant culture
> Case study: Advertising executives go to jail

For managers trying to build a legally compliant and ethically sound culture, it is gratifying to know that the steps to achieve one are exactly the same as the steps to achieve the other: ethics and legal compliance go hand in hand. LRN, a leading provider of governance, ethics and compliance management solutions, has outlined ten steps to achieving a more ethical and legally compliant culture.

1
Institute a code of conduct to verify and reinforce compliance to your programme.

2
Openly communicate an appropriate 'tone at the top'.

3
Market your compliance programme and make it relevant to your culture.

4
Assess key risks and map out risks for employees.

5
Educate employees on an ongoing basis.

6
Certify employee attestation to the programme.

7
Reward adherence to the 'letter and spirit' of the programme.

8
Promote self-reporting and clear channels of communication for quick detection of lapses.

9
Conduct compliance audits and benchmark results internally and externally.

10
Refine the programme on an ongoing basis by soliciting feedback from employees.

Relativity applies to physics, not ethics.

Albert Einstein
Theoretical physicist, philosopher and author

Ethics quiz

Donald Jugenheimer and Larry Kelley, in their book *Advertising Management*, offer a ten-question quiz for managers to make sure that they are approaching issues with ethical integrity:

1
'Have I gathered all the information I can find?

2
'Is the information biased in any way, for or against any course of action?

3
'Are all the right people involved in the process?

4
'Are any of the stakeholders trying to influence the outcome unduly?

5
'If I were one of the stakeholders, how would I react to each possible outcome or decision?

6
'Does the outcome match our institutional or corporate values and standards?

7
'Am I ashamed of this project or outcome, or trying to hide it in any way?

8
'Would the outcome be different if the situation were different?

9
'Would I be comfortable if this outcome became standard operating practice in our institution or firm?

10
'Is the outcome fair to everyone, or at least as fair as can be?'

Tony Miller, former executive vice president of LRN, stated: 'Generally, laws and standards of what is considered ethical workplace behaviour are common across industries.' He also noted that a big challenge for managers is the incentive and reward structures of most companies: 'Too often, substantial bonuses are tied to earnings targets, which are easy to measure, while the ability to foster an open culture... is not so easy to assess.'

A manager will only be successful in achieving a truly ethical and legally compliant culture if they factor appropriate behaviour into employee appraisals and reward systems.[1]

Case study: Advertising executives go to jail

Below is an excerpt from an *Adweek* magazine article. It outlines the realization of a company's worst nightmare. Ogilvy & Mather's executives were indicted and found guilty of fraud for over-billing the US Office of National Drug Control Policy (ONDCP):

'*Former Ogilvy & Mather (O&M) executive, Shona Seifert, today was sentenced in US District Court here to 18 months imprisonment (and two years probation) for her role in a scheme to over-bill the government's $1 billion [£700 million] Office of National Drug Control Policy (ONDCP) account to cover a $3 million [£1.9 million] revenue shortfall on the business.*

'*Seifert must also pay a $125,000 [£78,000] fine and a $1,000 [£625] special assessment, as well as write a "code of ethics" for the ad industry as part of 400 hours of community service.*

'*The case, said Judge Richard M. Berman, was essentially about the "slippage in ethics, and perhaps the absence of a code of ethics." Berman did not specify exactly what should be covered in that code, or how long it should be. It should be written by the time her probation ends.*

'*Berman said he read more than 70 letters of support that characterized Seifert as a "hugely successful, high-level executive," but noted that "success in business is illusory unless it is grounded in ethical business practices and those need to be... instilled in all of the workforce from the top to the bottom."*

'*In a tear-choked statement read before the court, Seifert called the five years during which she was investigated and tried "an absolute nightmare," and said she was "truly sorry" for the pain she had caused her family and husband.*'[2]

In addition to Seifert, O&M's former financial director, Thomas Early, was sentenced to 14 months imprisonment and two years probation in addition to paying $11,000 (£6,900) in fines and fees. The pair were convicted specifically for instructing employees to inflate the number of billable hours that they had worked on the government's anti-drug advertising. One of the most damning pieces of evidence against Seifert was an internal email stating: 'I'll wring the money out of them (the ONDCP). I promise.'

An ethical compass

This article should be truly frightening for any manager or potential manager to read. From all accounts, Seifert and Early were successful and talented managers, yet they perhaps lacked a clear ethical compass, which doomed their careers and ultimately impinged upon their liberty.

These executives are not unique. On a regular basis, corporate executives are found guilty of such things as rigging bids and falsifying reports. They also have another thing in common: almost invariably, they staunchly defend their actions. They paint themselves as scapegoats who are just doing 'business as usual'. In fact, when Seifert delivered her court-ordered code of ethics, it was dedicated to 'frontliners everywhere'. She wrote: 'If you are a frontliner, you are more likely to find yourself in the line of fire. And it may be better for others if you take a bullet.'[3] Even in the face of a unanimous guilty verdict and a prison sentence, it seems that her focus was on how she had been victimized, as opposed to her seemingly inconsistent ethical approach and the victimization of both her staff and her client.

If we apply the simple rules we have learned in this chapter, it is easy to see that things could have, and perhaps should have, turned out very differently for Seifert and Early.

Question 1
What steps would you recommend O&M take on a company-wide basis to ensure that this sort of unethical behaviour does not happen again?

Question 2
As part of her sentence, Seifert was asked to write a code of ethics for the advertising industry. Was this a good or a bad idea?

Question 3
When Seifert talks about 'frontliners' who 'take a bullet', does that make you believe that her actions were an anomaly or part of a wider ethical problem at the company?

Questions and exercises

>

Discussion questions

1
Are there times when a company's
financial survival overrides
ethical considerations?

2
If voluntary compliance is just that –
voluntary – why might a company
want to scrupulously avoid any
deviation from voluntary standards?

3
If employee and management
education is critical to compliance,
how often do you think internal
training should happen to help
guarantee compliance?

Exercises

1
Look at the ten items in the ethics
quiz on page 155. Rank them in
terms of which ones you think are
most important.

2
Look up Nestlé's code of conduct
on their website www.nestle.com.
Does it cover every ethical issue?
Do you think that anything is missing?

3
Assume that you are starting a
new company and that your code of
conduct can have only two items.
What would they be?

Summary

Success in marketing and management is often measured in financial terms, as it should be. However, all the financial success in the world rings hollow unless we work in a way that is both fair and that contributes something to society.

Ethical issues are not always that clear cut, so it is important for management to provide well-articulated corporate values that allow employees to do the right thing every day. Legal regulation is more clear cut, but it is important for companies, managers and employees to actively comply with regulation – and realize that doing so makes them better – rather than trying to skirt unpopular or unprofitable rules or regulations.

Suggested further reading

Jeffrey L. Seglin (2000) *The Good, the Bad, and Your Business: Choosing Right When Ethical Dilemmas Pull You Apart*. (Maine: Smith/Kerr Associates)

Laura Hartman (2002) *Perspectives in Business Ethics*. (New York: McGraw Hill)

John P. Kotter and James L. Heskett (1992) *Corporate Culture and Performance*. (New York: Simon and Schuster)

One common theme of business writers and philosophers is their recognition of the high amount of randomness in the world. While no book on business and management can make the world a less random place, I hope that this one can give you the tools to control those things that can be easily controlled in the workplace. I hope that it will also help to ensure that the truly random things that happen in the workplace have maximum impact when they are positive and minimum impact when they are negative.

I like to call my philosophy one of 'applied serendipity'. When we create a corporate culture that protects its core values relentlessly, while consistently encouraging managers and employees to push the envelope and to try new things, we have the best chance to create a sustainable company that is good for society.

A company that is good for society is one that inspires its employees, protects its customers, cares about the future of the planet, grows consistently year after year, and makes a lot of money doing it. Capitalism is about making money. We should not be ashamed of that: in fact, we should recognize its benefits. As we learned from the economic stagnation of Eastern Europe in the 20th century, lack of a profit motive means the production of fewer resources; fewer resources mean less for everybody, especially those less privileged.

Capitalism is an incredibly powerful force. The question is: what kind of impact are companies having while they make their money?

My friend and colleague, Adam Werbach, made the transition from full-time environmentalist to sustainability consultant for businesses worldwide. For someone who was the youngest ever president of the oldest environmental organization in the United States (The Sierra Club) and a worldwide board member of Greenpeace, this could possibly be considered a sell-out.

However, what Adam noted was how tremendously powerful the corporate sector is. And when that power is pointed in the right direction, its impact can be truly awesome. After he had tried, unsuccessfully, as an environmentalist to get New Orleans to fortify its wetlands and rebuild levees in the late 1990s (he was given a ceremonial key to the city for his efforts, but achieved little else), he watched, crestfallen, as the Hurricane Katrina disaster unfolded less than ten years later.

The experience gave him an epiphany:

'As I kept watching the news, I noticed that supplies from Wal-Mart seemed to reach the victims faster than the federal government's aid. Then the… big idea hit me: the corporate sector has the incentives, operational know-how, scalability, and ingenuity to respond to the global challenges we face today, challenges on all four fronts – social, economic, environmental and cultural.'

After reading this book, I hope that you have some new tools to ensure your success as a manager. I hope that, like me, you will be inspired by the words of Adam Werbach and will put them to the best use, for all of us.

Good management is the art of making problems so interesting and their solutions so constructive that everyone wants to get to work and deal with them.

Paul Hawken
Environmentalist, entrepreneur,
journalist and author

Endnotes

Chapter 1

1
Darlin, D. (2010) Applause, Please, for Early Adopters. *The New York Times*. [online] Available at <www.nytimes.com/2010/05/09/business/09every.html>

2
Donnypip (2007) Is Nintendo Wii's Scarcity Hurting Demand? *Game Industry Weekly*. [online] Available at <http://mblog.lib.umich.edu/giw/archives/2007/02/is_nintendo_wii.html>

Chapter 2

1
Gallo, C. (2007) Employee Motivation the Ritz-Carlton Way. *Bloomberg Businessweek*. [online] Available at <www.businessweek.com/smallbiz/content/feb2008/sb20080229_347490.htm>

2
Reiss, R. (2009) How Ritz-Carlton Stays at the Top. [online] Available at <www.forbes.com/2009/10/30/simon-cooper-ritz-leadership-ceonetwork-hotels.html>

Chapter 3

1
INSEAD is one of the world's top business schools, based in Paris.

2 and 3
Kim, W. C. and R. Mauborgne. (2005) *Blue Ocean Strategy: How to Create Uncontested Market Space and Make the Competition Irrelevant*. (Boston: Harvard Business School Publishing)

4
Reeves, R. (1983) George Gallup's Nation of Numbers. *Esquire Magazine*, December

5
Byron, E. (2010) Wash Away Bad Hair Days. *Wall Street Journal*, 30 June

Chapter 4

1
Interbrand best global brands 2010 ranking.

2
Quick MBA. Positioning: As popularized by Al Ries and Jack Trout. [online] <www.quickmba.com/marketing/ries-trout/positioning>

3
Moriarity, S., N. Mitchell and W. Wells. (2009) *Advertising Principles and Practices*. (New Jersey: Pearson Prentice Hall)

4
Dovel, G. P. (1990) Stake It Out: Positioning Success, Step by Step. *Business Marketing,* July

5
Hiam, A. (1991) *The Vest Pocket Marketer*. (New Jersey: Prentice Hall)

6
Roberts, K. (2006) *Lovemarks: The Future Beyond Brands*. (New York: powerHouse Books)

7
Sisodia, R. and J. Sheth, D. Wolfe (2007). *Firms of Endearment: How World-Class Companies Profit from Passion and Purpose*. (New Jersey: Wharton School Publishing)

8
Morgan, A. (2009) Eating the Big Fish: How Challenger Brands Can Compete Against Brand Leaders (New York: Wiley & Sons)

9
Gomelsky, V. (2003) paragraph 4, cited in Blackburn, S. (2004). Tiffany & Company: A Case Study. [online] <http://smu.edu/ecenter/discourse/blackburn.htm>

10
Gomelsky, V. (2003) paragraph 39 cited in Blackburn, S. (2004). Tiffany & Company: A Case Study. [online] <http://smu.edu/ecenter/discourse/blackburn.htm>

12
Lorge, S. (1998) paragraph 12, cited in Blackburn, S. (2004). Tiffany & Company: A Case Study. [online] <http://smu.edu/ecenter/discourse/blackburn.htm>

13
Associated Press (2010) Tiffany Reiterates 2010 Expansion Plan. *Businessweek*. [online] <www.businessweek.com/ap/financialnews/D9GD8A700.htm>

Chapter 5

1
Lockheed Martin, Corporate Vision and Value Statements [online] <www.lockheedmartin.com/aboutus/ethics/VisionValueStatements.html>

2
Rapaille, C. (2006) *The Culture Code: An Ingenious Way to Understand Why People Around the World Buy and Live as They Do* (New York: Random House)

3
Detert, J.R., E.R Burris and D.A. Harrison (2010) Debunking Four Myths About Employee Silence. *Harvard Business Review.* [online] <http://hbr.org/2010/06/debunking-four-myths-about-employee-silence/ar/1>

4
Heathfield, S.M. (2009) Workplace Conflict Resolution: People Management Tips. *Water Well Journal.* [online] <http://info.ngwa.org/GWOL/pdf/092583681.pdf>

5
Baksh-Mohammed, S. (2009) Managing Conflict. In: Jugenheimer, D. W. and Kelley L. D. (2009) *Advertising Management* (New York: M.E. Sharpe Inc.)

Chapter 6

1
Johnson, V. and S. C. Peppas. (2003). Crisis Management in Belgium: the case of Coca-Cola. *Corporate Communications: An International Journal*, 8, 1

2
O'Boyle, T. F. (1998) *At any cost: Jack Welch, General Electric, and the pursuit of profit (New York: Vintage)*

3
Welch, J. (2005) *Winning: The Ultimate Business How-to Book. (New York: HarperCollins)*

4 and 5
Moriarty, S., Mitchell, N. and W. Wells. (2005). *Advertising Principles and Practices.* (Harlow: Prentice Hall)

6
Lukaszewski, J. E. (1998) Seven Dimensions of Crisis Communication Management: A Strategic Analysis and Planning Model. *Ragan's Communications Journal* (Jan/Feb 1999)

7
Jacques, A. (2009) Domino's delivers during crisis. *The Public Relations Strategist* [online] <www.prsa.org/Intelligence/TheStrategist/Articles/view/8226/102/Domino_s_delivers_during_crisis_The_company_s_step>

8
Carroll, C. (2009) Defying a Reputational Crisis – Cadbury's Salmonella Scare. *Corporate Reputational Review* [online] <www.palgrave-journals.com/crr/journal/v12/n1/full/crr200834a.html>

Chapter 7

1
Tilbian, L. (2005) WPP at 20. *Campaign* [online] <http://campaignlive.co.uk/news/473477/WPP-Twenty>

2
Corstjens M. and J. Merrihue (2003) in: Young, A. and L. Aitkin. (2007). *Profitable Marketing Communications: A Guide to Marketing Return on Investment.* (London: Kogan Page)

Chapter 8

1
Weiss, S. (2005) The Ethical Side of Compliance. *Information Week* [online] <www.informationweek.com/news/showArticle.jhtml?articleID=165701054>

2
Zammit, D. (2005) Seifert's Sentence. *Adweek* [online] <www.adweek.com/aw/esearch/article_display.jsp?vnu_content_id=1000979190>

3
(2005) Convicted Seifert Urges 'No Compromise' in Ad Industry Ethics Code. *Media Week* [online] <www.mediaweek.co.uk/news/504294/Convicted-Seifert-urges-no-compromise-ad-industry-ethics-code>

All online articles accessed 4 February 2011.

Index

Compiled by Indexing Specialists (UK) Ltd.

Picture credits

All reasonable attempts have been made to trace, clear and credit the copyright holders of the images reproduced in this book. However, if any credits have been inadvertently omitted, the publisher will endeavour to incorporate amendments in future editions.

Page 3
Mad Men, courtesy of AMC, The Kobal Collection.

Page 15
Wall Street (1987), courtesy of 20th Century Fox, The Kobal Collection.

Page 27
Google Maps with Street View © 2010 Google. All rights reserved.

Page 33
PlugTail poster © 2008 Pass & Seymour/Legrand.

Page 35
British Airways' Club World courtesy of Newscast.

Page 37
Volcano image © Johann Helgason. Courtesy of Shutterstock.com.

Page 43
Star Trek, courtesy of Paramount Television, The Kobal Collection.

Page 47
Post-it note image © Jacob Bøtter.

Page 48
Nelson Mandela, South Africa, 1999 © Abbas/Magnum Photos.

Page 57
Ritz-Carlton Hotel, Doha, Qatar © Stepnout.

Page 65
Cirque du Soleil © Joel Ryan/Press Association.

Page 75
One in a Billion © powerHouse Books.

Page 79
Apple iPad image © 2011 Apple Inc. All rights reserved.

Page 87
Chick-fil-A image. Chick-fil-A Stylized®, Eat Mor Chikin®, and the Chick-fil-A Cows® are registered trademarks of CFA Properties, Inc.

Page 93
Breakfast at Tiffany's poster, courtesy of Paramount, The Kobal Collection.

Page 95
Blue boxes image © Natalia Bratslavsky. Courtesy of Shutterstock.

Page 106
Petrobras Magazine © Petrobras – 2009.

Page 125
Crisis Management cartoon © 2004 by Randy Glasbergen. www.glasbergen.com.

Page 139
Google analytics page. © 2010 Google. All rights reserved.

Page 145
Copyright © 1995–2009 Samsung. All rights reserved.

Page 151
The Beverly Hillbillies. © CBS TV/The Kobal Collection.

Acknowledgements

The author would like to thank the following for their help with the book:

Antony Young
Bill Cochrane
Bob Seelert
Clare Sheehan
Clare Slattery
Danny Burke
Daria Sheehan
David Shaw
Ed Russell
Georgia Kennedy
Hank Sheehan
James Tsao
Janie Sheehan
John Favalo
John Philip Jones
Julie Halpin
Karen Greenfield
Kate Sheehan
Kathy Sheehan
Kevin O'Neill
Kevin Roberts
Kevin Sheehan
Larry Elin
Lorraine Branham
Maria Fong Sheehan
Matt Murphy
Milano Reyna
Nilla Sheehan
Ruth Slattery
Sandy Thompson
Steve Masiclat
Wayne Keeley
William G. Sheehan Jr.
William G. Sheehan Sr.

BASICS
MARKETING

Working with ethics

Lynne Elvins
Naomi Goulder

Publisher's note

The subject of ethics is not new, yet its consideration within the applied visual arts is perhaps not as prevalent as it might be. Our aim here is to help a new generation of students, educators and practitioners find a methodology for structuring their thoughts and reflections in this vital area.

AVA Publishing hopes that these **Working with ethics** pages provide a platform for consideration and a flexible method for incorporating ethical concerns in the work of educators, students and professionals. Our approach consists of four parts:

The **introduction** is intended to be an accessible snapshot of the ethical landscape, both in terms of historical development and current dominant themes.

The **framework** positions ethical consideration into four areas and poses questions about the practical implications that might occur. Marking your response to each of these questions on the scale shown will allow your reactions to be further explored by comparisons.

The **case study** sets out a real project and then poses some ethical questions for further consideration. This is a focus point for a debate rather than a critical analysis so there are no predetermined right or wrong answers.

A selection of **further reading** for you to consider areas of particular interest in more detail.

Ethical: awareness/ reflection/ debate

Introduction

Ethics is a complex subject that interlaces the idea of responsibilities to society with a wide range of considerations relevant to the character and happiness of the individual. It concerns virtues of compassion, loyalty and strength, but also of confidence, imagination, humour and optimism. As introduced in ancient Greek philosophy, the fundamental ethical question is: *what should I do?* How we might pursue a 'good' life not only raises moral concerns about the effects of our actions on others, but also personal concerns about our own integrity.

In modern times the most important and controversial questions in ethics have been the moral ones. With growing populations and improvements in mobility and communications, it is not surprising that considerations about how to structure our lives together on the planet should come to the forefront. For visual artists and communicators, it should be no surprise that these considerations will enter into the creative process.

Some ethical considerations are already enshrined in government laws and regulations or in professional codes of conduct. For example, plagiarism and breaches of confidentiality can be punishable offences. Legislation in various nations makes it unlawful to exclude people with disabilities from accessing information or spaces. The trade of ivory as a material has been banned in many countries. In these cases, a clear line has been drawn under what is unacceptable.

But most ethical matters remain open to debate, among experts and lay-people alike, and in the end we have to make our own choices on the basis of our own guiding principles or values. Is it more ethical to work for a charity than for a commercial company? Is it unethical to create something that others find ugly or offensive?

Specific questions such as these may lead to other questions that are more abstract. For example, is it only effects on humans (and what they care about) that are important, or might effects on the natural world require attention too?

Is promoting ethical consequences justified even when it requires ethical sacrifices along the way? Must there be a single unifying theory of ethics (such as the Utilitarian thesis that the right course of action is always the one that leads to the greatest happiness of the greatest number), or might there always be many different ethical values that pull a person in various directions?

As we enter into ethical debate and engage with these dilemmas on a personal and professional level, we may change our views or change our view of others. The real test though is whether, as we reflect on these matters, we change the way we act as well as the way we think. Socrates, the 'father' of philosophy, proposed that people will naturally do 'good' if they know what is right. But this point might only lead us to yet another question: *how do we know what is right?*

You
What are your ethical beliefs?

Central to everything you do will be your attitude to people and issues around you. For some people, their ethics are an active part of the decisions they make every day as a consumer, a voter or a working professional. Others may think about ethics very little and yet this does not automatically make them unethical. Personal beliefs, lifestyle, politics, nationality, religion, gender, class or education can all influence your ethical viewpoint.

Using the scale, where would you place yourself? What do you take into account to make your decision? Compare results with your friends or colleagues.

Your client
What are your terms?

Working relationships are central to whether ethics can be embedded into a project, and your conduct on a day-to-day basis is a demonstration of your professional ethics. The decision with the biggest impact is whom you choose to work with in the first place. Cigarette companies or arms traders are often-cited examples when talking about where a line might be drawn, but rarely are real situations so extreme. At what point might you turn down a project on ethical grounds and how much does the reality of having to earn a living affect your ability to choose?

Using the scale, where would you place a project? How does this compare to your personal ethical level?

01 02 03 04 05 06 07 08 09 10

01 02 03 04 05 06 07 08 09 10

Your specifications
What are the impacts of your materials?

In relatively recent times, we are learning that many natural materials are in short supply. At the same time, we are increasingly aware that some man-made materials can have harmful, long-term effects on people or the planet. How much do you know about the materials that you use? Do you know where they come from, how far they travel and under what conditions they are obtained? When your creation is no longer needed, will it be easy and safe to recycle? Will it disappear without a trace? Are these considerations your responsibility or are they out of your hands?

Using the scale, mark how ethical your material choices are.

Your creation
What is the purpose of your work?

Between you, your colleagues and an agreed brief, what will your creation achieve? What purpose will it have in society and will it make a positive contribution? Should your work result in more than commercial success or industry awards? Might your creation help save lives, educate, protect or inspire? Form and function are two established aspects of judging a creation, but there is little consensus on the obligations of visual artists and communicators toward society, or the role they might have in solving social or environmental problems. If you want recognition for being the creator, how responsible are you for what you create and where might that responsibility end?

Using the scale, mark how ethical the purpose of your work is.

01 02 03 04 05 06 07 08 09 10

01 02 03 04 05 06 07 08 09 10

One aspect of marketing that raises an ethical dilemma is the extent to which marketing techniques might persuade or influence consumers to purchase items that they may not need or that may even be detrimental. Central to this question is the balance of power in the relationship between the seller and the buyer. Marketers emphasise the positive attributes of a product or service and cement favourable associations in the minds of the target audience, usually to generate sales. In free markets, buyers should be able to compare and choose from a variety of competitive options. However, as marketing has become increasingly diverse in its formats and complex in its application of psychological techniques, questions can be raised about the freedom of individuals to choose fairly.
Do marketers genuinely feel positive about the products and services that they help to promote, or are they driven purely to make profit for themselves and the seller? Should marketers take responsibility for ensuring that buyers can make fully informed choices? Or is this issue already taken care of through independent consumer groups and anti-trust law?

Social marketing has become increasingly popular among governments and campaign groups as a way of addressing serious health issues, particularly in developing countries. The global HIV/AIDS epidemic is stabilising, but it is still at an unacceptably high level. According to UNAIDS figures, an estimated 33 million people across the globe were living with HIV in 2007, around 22 million of whom resided in sub-Saharan Africa.

Although not the only method of prevention available, the male latex condom is the most efficient and readily available technology capable of reducing the sexual transmission of HIV and other sexually transmitted infections. In the mid 1980s, the social marketing of condoms emerged as an effective tool in the fight to combat the spread of HIV/AIDS. Programmes made condoms available, affordable and acceptable in countries affected by the epidemic and used marketing messages to raise awareness of the disease.

One marketing technique that might be deployed is to recruit prominent individuals and groups to deliver and endorse safer sex messages. This approach has been successful through the recruitment of sports and music figures, religious leaders and politicians.

In 1996, Archbishop Tutu delivered an impassioned plea for South Africans to face the facts about HIV/AIDS in a television documentary entitled 'The Rubber Revolution'. Tutu, along with other religious leaders and various national sports figures, discussed the importance of open conversations about sexuality and HIV/AIDS. Prior to Tutu's involvement, the South African Broadcasting Corporation had not allowed the word 'condom' to be used on primetime television.

With support from USAID and other non-profit organisations, the condom brand Prudence was introduced to Zaire in 1996. Previous to this campaign, the total number of condoms given away or sold in Zaire was approximately 500,000 a year. In 1999, four million Prudence condoms were sold. A key tactic in the marketing campaign was the placement and pricing strategy. By selling Prudence condoms via street hawkers at three cents each, people were able to get hold of condoms anywhere at any time. Salespeople were also supported with Prudence key rings, bartender aprons, calendars, hats and signs; and music events offered half-price admission to anyone with a Prudence pack. The marketing campaign has been so successful that Zairians now use 'Prudence' as a generic term for a condom.

Is it more ethical to practise social marketing than commercial marketing?

Is it unethical to pay somebody to endorse a product or service that they do not use?

Would you work on a project to market condoms in African countries?

There is an increasing political and social consensus that something needs to be done to safeguard children from the worst excesses of direct marketing and the pressures of commercialisation.

Reverend Dr Rowan Williams
The Archbishop of Canterbury

Further reading

AIGA
Design Business and Ethics
2007, AIGA

Eaton, Marcia Muelder
Aesthetics and the Good Life
1989, Associated University Press

Ellison, David
Ethics and Aesthetics in European Modernist Literature:
From the Sublime to the Uncanny
2001, Cambridge University Press

Fenner, David E W (Ed)
Ethics and the Arts:
An Anthology
1995, Garland Reference Library of Social Science

Gini, Al and Marcoux, Alexei M
Case Studies in Business Ethics
2005, Prentice Hall

McDonough, William and Braungart, Michael
Cradle to Cradle:
Remaking the Way We Make Things
2002, North Point Press

Papanek, Victor
Design for the Real World:
Making to Measure
1972, Thames & Hudson

United Nations Global Compact
The Ten Principles
www.unglobalcompact.org/AboutTheGC/TheTenPrinciples/index.html